CREATING YOUR DIGITAL PORTFOLIO

For more excellent books and resources for
designers, visit www.howdesign.com.

14 13 12 11 10   5 4 3 2 1

Distributed in Canada by Fraser Direct
100 Armstrong Avenue
Georgetown, Ontario, Canada L7G 5S4
Tel: (905) 877-4411

Library of Congress Cataloging-in-Publication Data

ISBN 10: 1-4403-1023-8
ISBN 13: 978-1-4403-1023-2

DISCLAIMER: The advice offered in this book is
for informational purposes only. Consult a legal
professional for actionable advice.

Art direction: Tony Seddon
Design concept: Emily Portnoi
Page layout: Rebecca Stephenson
Typeset in Verdana, Delta Jaeger, and Kontrapunkt

Printed in China by 1010 Printing International Ltd.

For my father

CREATING YOUR DIGITAL PORTFOLIO

The Essential Guide to Showcasing Your Design Work Online

IAN CLAZIE

HOW BOOKS
Cincinnati, Ohio
www.howdesign.com

Contents

GOING LIVE   144

MAINTENANCE   178

Introduction

The aim of this book is to help graphic designers, illustrators, and other creative professionals navigate the challenge of creating a digital portfolio. It contains practical advice to getting your work into a portable digital format ready to share on the web. It also discusses the thinking behind creating a portfolio, your objectives, and communication strategy.

There is a second purpose at play here; the book also serves as a catalog of carefully chosen example portfolios for inspiration and reference. Some of the examples are portfolios of individuals and some are design studio websites, but the lessons to be learned from these sites are universal.

Simply put, this book is about building effective digital portfolios. The better your portfolio is, the easier your interviews with prospective employers and clients will be.

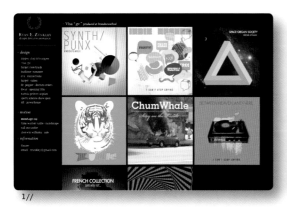

1//

2//

Maybe you're still wondering, why go digital? There are many benefits to having a digital portfolio. It means that anyone can access your work at any time, making it highly portable. A quick email from one reviewer to another is all it takes to spread word of your capabilities, creativity, and contact information.

Other advantages include the ability to change details and content rapidly and easily without having to redistribute any physical material. You also gain the ability to link to relevant information, websites, live projects, and collaborators online.

Having a digital portfolio can also help to modernize your personal brand, as it demonstrates a working knowledge of digital communications and technology. In most instances, appearing to be up-to-date can depict a favorable image to a potential employer or client.

3//

Depending on what you are trying to achieve, the capacity to generate "organic" traffic to your portfolio site may be essential. Organic traffic is considered to be visits from people who come across your site via a search engine or by following a link from another site. We'll discuss ways to stimulate organic traffic and digital conversations that can benefit your business goals.

Your portfolio is like a stage. The moment before it is reviewed is like the moment before the curtain opens. Your audience doesn't know what to expect. If the work you showcase is the play itself, then your portfolio is the stage and sets. Having a traditional non-digital portfolio is a bit like having your stage located in a small town only as big as you're able to walk across. Having a digital portfolio is more like having it in Times Square.

1// Ryan Zunkley,
ryanzunkley.com

2// Adam Rix,
adamrix.com

3// GrandArmy,
grand-army.com

What's particularly exciting about showcasing your work on the web is that great creativity gets noticed and talked about more readily there. It may not happen overnight, but if your work is unique, inspiring, or thought-provoking, putting it out on the web will eventually lead to comments, conversations, collaborations, and clients.

To get there, first we'll develop a strategy; then we'll use smart tactics to implement the strategy and build a digital portfolio. We will discuss the right approach for filling a portfolio with your work, and finally we'll explore ways to get the most out of your portfolio. Hopefully you will find the advice practical and inspiring and will end up with a professional and useful digital portfolio that communicates the right message about you.

The contents of this book can be sliced another way: it offers help with creating a professional digital portfolio quickly and easily for those who don't need to reinvent the wheel, and help with, well... reinventing the wheel.

It's important to cover the basics and cover them well, then get creative and really dive in. If you are naturally prone to getting into things over your head then this book will explain ways to keep you from drowning completely.

Creating a portfolio and putting your work on display can be an anxious experience. Often you'll wonder what people really think when they view your site. Are they holding back on their true reaction? This is where the thinking behind what you're trying to do can really help. If you start the process by asking yourself some basic questions—questions that we'll cover in the first section of this book—you should find it easier to take feedback on board and handle potential rejection if and when you don't get hired for that dream job.

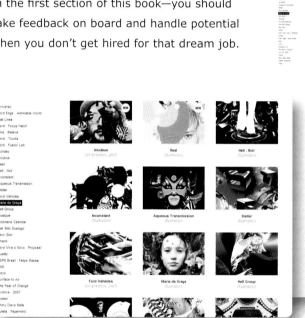

3//

This book is meant to inspire as well as instruct. Don't let all the technical bits slow you down if you are feeling fired up and ready to dive in. Trying to follow every recommendation in this book is probably impossible. That said, knowing what rules you are breaking and when can be helpful. Setting specific and measurable goals for yourself will pave the way for important decisions you will need to make. Let's begin with the question, "What do you want to achieve?"

1// Jan Pautsch.Lilienthal,
thismortalmagic.com

2// Trevor Van Meter,
tvmstudio.com

3// Danilo Rodrigues,
cargocollective.com/danilorodrigues

Chapter One:
Develop a strategy

Chapter Two:
Implement your strategy

STRATEGY

Forming a strategy for your digital portfolio is an important step if you want to get the most out of the end result. To achieve your goals, you need to create something that is going to help you connect with your target audience. Gaining insight into your industry and your potential employers and clients is a good place to start your research.

When building a digital portfolio, you will find it can be useful to cover the essentials first before reaching beyond the boundaries. We'll discuss what these essentials are and then move on to the details of digital user experience design, some technical considerations, and finally the means to take things further creatively.

CHAPTER ONE: Develop a strategy
Know your industry

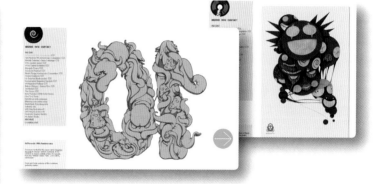

Creating your own portfolio is a bit like any other creative project you might undertake. There are certain essential pieces of information that your "brief" must contain. As you are both designer and client on this project, you will need to answer the following question for yourself: Who is your target audience?

To create an effective portfolio, you will need a strategy that is informed by insights into what your prospective employers are about and what they are looking for. You need to figure out:

1. What are they expecting to see for the type of role or project you are aiming for? (What's the baseline that absolutely needs to be covered?)
2. What will likely surprise them in a good way? (How can you knock their socks off so you stand out from the crowd?)

To gain some insight about where your target audience is coming from, you must have an idea of what type of work you're looking for and what industry sector it lies in. Knowing the context in which your potential employers operate will help you form your strategy.

How is this thinking applied practically? Here are some questions to reflect on when considering the people you wish to target:

1. Is their world energetic and chaotic, or subdued and reflective?
2. Do they operate in a realm where quality and craft are held above all else, or do commercial impact, practicality, and clear communication rank highest in priority?
3. How far off the beaten path does your particular targeted industry sector sit, and what price do they put on originality versus tried-and-true competent execution?

2//

For example, imagine you are an illustrator looking for editorial work with quirky and unique handcrafted periodicals. Your target art director likely has the perspective that originality is a high priority.

By contrast, if you are a graphic designer looking for corporate print design including annual reports, a key part of your strategy will be to emphasize your professionalism and accountability.

If the industry sectors you are targeting encompass a wide range of contexts, consider a strategy based around flexibility, ease of navigation, and clear information about your work and the roles you have played on collaborative projects to be sure your reviewers can easily find the work samples relevant to them.

1// *Michele Angelo,*
superexpresso.com
This Barcelona-based designer places emphasis on unique, high-quality craftsmanship to attract clients looking for something new.

2// *Monica Brand and Francisco López, mogollon-ny.com*
Demonstrating your work in multiple contexts can indicate an ability to own a project completely and inspires confidence in your ability to follow through.

Know your CDs, ADs, and DDs

Once you have done some research into your target audience's environment, consider the individuals themselves. Good designers of websites always make an effort to put themselves in the shoes of those who will use their sites. Browsing a website is different from reading a book or magazine or watching television. When someone is at their computer, with distractions like the massive amount of information and entertainment on the web and the constant stream of communication via email, instant messaging, and other means, they are most challenged for attention and focus.

You have literally fractions of a second to make the right first impression on a prospective employer. Creative directors, art directors, design directors, and direct clients generally have one trait in common: if they are looking to hire someone, it's partly because they have more work than they can handle and are extremely busy. This shortens the attention span even further.

What does this mean for your portfolio?

- Make the first impression count.
- Put your best work up front.
- Make it easy for a visitor to find their way around.
- Make it easy for them to learn about your abilities and roles.
- Make it easy for them to contact you.

We will cover all of these aspects in detail in this book.

1//

So, if those qualities hold true for most hiring professionals across all industries, how about the specific individuals that you're targeting? If you are looking for work in an agency environment, it pays to know how agencies are structured. Do you know the difference between a creative director and an art director in the type of agency you are targeting? What exactly is a design director?

In most contexts, a creative director is responsible for overall ideation, communication, and creative strategy. Art and design directors are responsible for the execution of the ideas, messaging, and strategy. The difference between an art director and a design director is open to interpretation; however, an art director, in an advertising context at least, quite often comes from a copywriting or creative ideation background, whereas a design director would most likely have held a senior designer position previously.

If you are applying for an open role in an agency, think about who is likely to be reviewing candidates for that role and consider their likely background and orientation. If you are looking for work directly with clients, the range of perspectives is even greater. One client may have you working directly with a marketing communications-oriented professional. Another may see you dealing with someone in human resources. The wider the audience type, the more need for flexibility, usability, and clear messaging. Bear in mind that if your target is to reach direct clients, a broad and slightly more neutral approach may be most practical in generating more business than an approach that emphasizes your originality and ability to think off the beaten path.

2//

1// Firstborn,
firstbornmultimedia.com
When you know your audience you can speak to them directly. In Firstborn's case, the audience is direct clients who need to know they're hiring a leader in their field.

2// Hello Monday,
hellomonday.net
Like Hello Monday, consider referring to sources of inspiration in the descriptions of your work to indicate the level of thinking that you put into your projects.

Create your elevator pitch

Your elevator pitch is a description of what you do in the most direct terms possible. In some cases it will be a description of what you would like to do, or what you would like to get paid to do. In this way your pitch may function as an objective statement.

Writing a clear objective statement is a little like the challenge a startup company faces in defining its business model. Good advice is to cut to the chase in describing where your focus lies. It only takes a moment before someone has enough question marks in their head that they decide to move on. These question marks arise from not knowing what you do and what you can do for them.

1//

Write a statement you believe in and don't be afraid to put it right up front:

"Freelance graphic designer, illustrator, and cartoonist."
"Textile design, packaging design, and photography is what I do."
"Lots of vivid ideas, catchy design, and modern concepts are made here."

You should be able to describe what you do in twenty-five words or fewer. If you can't do this, you will struggle to catch the attention of someone who is time-poor and just wants to know if you are the one they should be looking into or not.

2//

Tech tip

Your portfolio's interface isn't the only place where your elevator pitch will come in handy for orienting visitors—HTML page titles are a good location as well. Placing an even more condensed version in between the <title> tags inside the <head> area in an HTML file will cause the text to appear at the top of the browser window, in the description of a shortcut or bookmark, and in Google search results.

Taking this one step further, you can put your full-length pitch into a <meta name="Description"... > tag, which will also get picked up by Google and will appear as the blurb beneath the link to your site in a page of search results. Ignore this bit of technology and search engines will look for whatever text they can find that may wind up being your site's navigation. Words like "portfolio," "about," and "contact" don't tell people much about where you are coming from and what you are looking to provide.

Quick tip

If the type of work you do requires that you meet face to face with clients, it is important to indicate your location up front. Consider adding it to the end of your objective statement. For example: "Graphic and packaging design in San Francisco." Making this extra information clear helps the right people find you quickly and easily.

1// *Juan Diego Velasco,*
juandiegovelasco.com
This website offers one of the
warmest welcomes of any
digital portfolio out there.

2// *Orman Clark,*
ormanclark.com
Direct and descriptive, this introduction
leaves few questions unanswered.

How will you use your portfolio?

A portfolio is like a tool in that it helps you create things. Generally speaking, it helps you create work opportunities. It is important to figure out what type of work opportunities you are trying to create with it to best inform what type of tool you need.

Here's a quick exercise: Answer the following to the best of your ability at this time. You may need to come back to this after doing a bit more thinking and research.

Do I intend to use my portfolio more like...
A) ...a direct mail piece...
B) ...or a business card?

Do I need something that...
A) ...generates its own audience...
B) ...or will I use this only for pointing specific
   people to?

Will I need to...
A) ...benefit from passersby to the site...
B) ...or will this essentially be an extension of
   my brand?

1//

If you answered more A than B, you may face a slightly more challenging road ahead. However, you will open your eyes to a whole new world—the realms of digital marketing and social networking. Be aware that any inroads you make here may require a little patience; in most cases, the greatest rewards kick in further down the track. Put another way, the more effort you put in, the more reward you are likely to get out.

If you answered more B than A, you may have a fairly simple task on your hands. You are most likely going to benefit from putting your work in one well-presented location that you can point individual reviewers to and pull up in an interview to walk through your work.

Examples of strategy-determining tactics:

If organic traffic is needed (scenario A), having a clear objective stated upfront becomes even more important. Incorporating a blog can help raise your search engine page ranking, which will have a snowballing effect on your traffic.

If you have a wide range of skills and need to customize your portfolio quickly to suit different pitches and interviews, this is an important consideration to identify upfront.

As we will see in the following sections, there are approaches that lend themselves more or less to ease of quick content changes. Some solutions, particularly highly conceptual handmade portfolios, can be difficult to update with different content quickly.

Quick tip

If you are positioning yourself for freelance work or setting up a business, it can be very important to have your own domain name (that is, "yourname. com"). If you are seeking employment it is less vital. Think of your web address as an extension of your brand. A specific benefit of a unique, concise, and memorable domain name is that your site will be easier for people to find, whether via word of mouth or by online search.

1// Guðmundur Bjarni Sigurðsson, gummisig.com
Example of a site that aims to generate interest from organic traffic (scenario A).

2// Sean Freeman, thereis.co.uk
Example of a site that does little to reach out to passersby and is more niche in its appeal (scenario B).

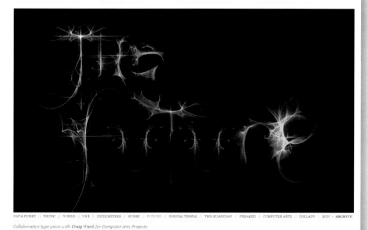

THERE IS // SHOWCASE
SEAN@THEREIS.CO.UK

FAT & FURRY // THINK! // WIRED // VH1 // ONZE METRES // SUISSE // FUTURE // DIGITAL TEMPLE // THE GUARDIAN // FREAKED // COMPUTER ARTS // INK LADY // BON - ARCHIVE
Collaborative type piece with Craig Ward for Computer Arts Projects.
* * * *

2//

Put clear messages on your site

Q: What are the essential ingredients of a successful portfolio?

"Keep it simple and elegant. Projects should be presented in one glance with a short note about the work, the task, the applicant's role, and a link if it's digital and not a lazy mishmash of references."

—Elke Klinkhammer, Creative Director, Neue Digitale, Germany

We've discussed how to come up with your elevator pitch and the importance of being able to state succinctly what you do and what your objectives are. Having clear messaging on your site—the information design that communicates your capabilities and objectives to passersby—is an essential ingredient for an effective portfolio.

1//

One approach could be:

1. Write down what you're good at.
2. Write down what you want to be good at.
3. Merge the two.
4. Now make it more concise.
5. Inject a bit of personality.
6. Proofread it.
7. Add it to your site in a prominent place so it is one of the first bits of information people read.

1// Ray Sison,
skilledconcept.com
You can't miss what this creative
professional's roles are.

2// Ronnie Wright,
ronniewright.co.uk
Here, clear messaging conveys not
only information, but personality too.

Having clear messaging on your website makes it easy for people to learn about you and what you can do for them.

Examples of objective statements that use clear messaging:

"Experienced London-based advertising art director with
 a graphic design background."

"Freelance illustrator in Chicago now available."

"Fashion photographer."

If this sounds too much like putting yourself in a box when you believe you're not box-able, that's fine. There are times when it is best to leave off the description of what you do because your work speaks for itself. For the majority of portfolios, however, it will help to have some simple, clear words to give visitors an easy way to begin their discovery of who you are, what you do, and whether they want to hire you.

Design tip

If you plan on using typographic design to integrate your elevator pitch into your interface, bear in mind the fundamentals of typographic and information design and be wary if these are not your particular strengths. Your work may be great, but if the design around your messaging is poor it will reflect badly on you. Stick to your strengths and consider the following as a guide:

1st in the information hierarchy: Your name.
2nd: Your simply stated elevator pitch, with no mistakes or ambiguity.
3rd: Your best work.
4th: Quick and easy access to the rest of your work and more information on your experience and abilities.

2//

Give clear descriptions of your work

Describing your work in the captions adjacent to each piece shown in your portfolio is a great opportunity to educate a reviewer about your capabilities and thought processes. You should include this important information:

1. Project title
2. Client name
3. Your role (and credits for other contributors)
4. The brief
5. Key insight
6. Your solution
7. Results
8. Relevant links

This may sound like a lot of information to include with each piece, but each of these points can be described very succinctly (the more succinct the better). A reviewer scanning a paragraph quickly is looking for key facts, not a novel.

1//

2//

3//

Consider this possible structure to get an idea of how these elements tie together:

- Project title
- Client name
- Your role
- The brief in as few words as possible. A key insight that sets up the next sentence, which will describe how you answered the brief. A quick sentence to sum up how you chose to solve this brief. A short mention of how the client felt about the work or how it performed if there is a way to measure this particular outcome.
- Link to a related website

For pieces that were created as personal projects, the same structure can apply and be equally effective:

- Project title
- Personal project
- Your role, etc

1// *Sean Freeman,*

thereis.co.uk

Descriptions can be very concise and still be effective.

2// *Firstborn,*

firstbornmultimedia.com

A more thorough approach.

3// *Wonderwall,*

wonder-wall.com

A consistent structure makes processing the information easier.

Create a professional-looking portfolio

The commercial realities that your potential employers face lead them to seek professional allies in meeting these challenges. One way to come across as reliable, switched on, and trustworthy is to make sure that your digital portfolio looks suitably clean, professional, and inviting. There are times for breaking all rules, this one included. But if you choose to break this rule, consider what the appearance of your portfolio says about what it would be like to employ you.

So exactly what is a professional appearance for a portfolio?

It's helpful to consider some real-world containers that house visual communication pieces for cues. What do portfolio folders and art galleries have in common? They tend to be clean, minimal, have muted colors, and are highly functional. They are like this so that the work stands out. These are tried-and-tested means of not having the packaging upstage the contents.

When is this rule worth breaking? When the package is a big part of the demonstration of your abilities. Use caution if you go down this path; there are some pitfalls, as we will discuss later in the book.

1//

2//

Design tip

A common mistake that non-digital designers make when creating their first digital interface is to place visual design above interaction design and usability. Your site needs to excel in both disciplines. Try to avoid great-looking interfaces that are confusing to use. Likewise, a highly usable but underwhelming interface isn't going to say much for your visual design taste and ability.

The core elements of a professional-looking web interface are:

1. Good typography
2. Usable and well-designed interface elements
3. Color and layout balance
4. Clear information hierarchy
5. Clear identity across the entire site, including your name in a consistent and prominent location

There are plenty of examples of professional-looking portfolio interfaces out there that are anything but boring. For just a few, visit *www.clazie.com/digitalportfolios.*

1// X3 Studios,
x3studios.com
X3 Studios portray professionalism through their use of bold typography and a clean interface.

2// Anton Repponen,
repponen.com
This minimalist but attractive and highly functional portfolio is hosted by the free online portfolio service Cargo Collective (see page 35).

Find a strong concept for your site

1//

If you are reading this page, it is because you are not satisfied with just covering the basics. You want to do something new, different, innovative, and unique. Good for you. Maybe the thought of having a portfolio that resembles anyone else's makes you cringe, or maybe you simply want to do everything you can to stand out from the crowd.

When you have landed on a good central idea, you will find that many of the design decisions you need to make along the way will come together cohesively. A good central idea provides a framework on which to hang your creative execution.

Where to start? Think up a central idea. Worked into an execution it will become a concept. At the very least you might consider a theme. Let's focus on zeroing in on a good concept.

What exactly is a concept and how do you get one? A concept can be many things. It could be a visual metaphor where the interface elements become props in a scene that mimics some aspect of real life. Or it could be something altogether alien. A concept can be whimsical, illustrative, minimal, or eclectic... The possibilities are endless.

To come up with an idea, first gather inspiration, and then aim for a bunch of ideas instead of one perfect idea. This helps take the pressure off. Remember that the brainstorming process should be a positive experience. If you are critical along the way, you will restrict the natural flow of ideas. Collect several sketchy possibilities and you will find that stepping away and coming back will trigger new ideas, which will in turn trigger more. You can always come back later to evaluate and weed out the weaker ones.

Some words of caution: The essentials we've just discussed are still just that—essentials—so don't turn your back on them. If you sacrifice any of those important points for the sake of showing how clever you can be, you might set off all kinds of alarm bells with reviewers. Whatever you do, make sure you revisit your original strategy to make sure you are not undermining your goals with a particular direction. But enough caution. Grab a pencil and start brainstorming. We will go into greater detail on the process of ideas generation in Chapter Two.

2//

3//

1// Dave Werner,

okaydave.com

A scrapbook visual metaphor brings

a warm and tactile quality to this site.

2// Darek Nyckowiak,

thetoke.com

Darek's site employs multiple display

modes in three dimensions to create

a compelling experience.

3// Scott Hansen,

iso50.com

Scott's work is nostalgic and

thoughtfully crafted, as is his

site's interface design.

Grab your audience

First impressions really count. You have only a fraction of a second to make a splash in the mind of a reviewer. Make sure you put your best work upfront, or, if your intention is to be innovative with your portfolio design, do something that will really get their attention.

One way to create visual impact is to lead off with a motion reel (a video summary) of your work. This can be challenging to create if you don't have the necessary skills, but when done well the effect is impressive. A motion reel is not much of a stretch if your work involves motion graphics, animation, or interactive design, as these media lend themselves naturally to presentation in video form.

Static graphic design and illustration can be presented as video using motion graphics techniques to form transitions between pieces combined with typographic labels. Set it to music that complements your style and you're ready to embed the video at the front door of your site.

Flash animation can be used to create visual impact in interactive motion and an interface that seems to be alive, responding to every rollover and click of the mouse. Create a cheesy intro animation of poor quality and you will fall victim to the dreaded "skip intro" disease—visitors will be put off and scramble for a button to take them straight through to your work, if they don't turn away entirely.

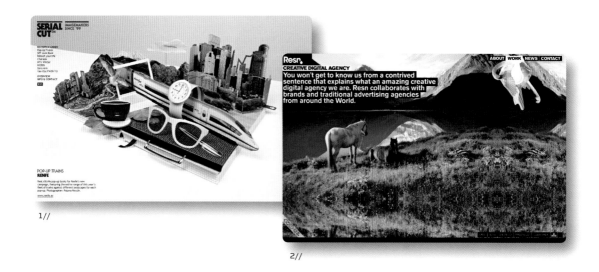

1//

2//

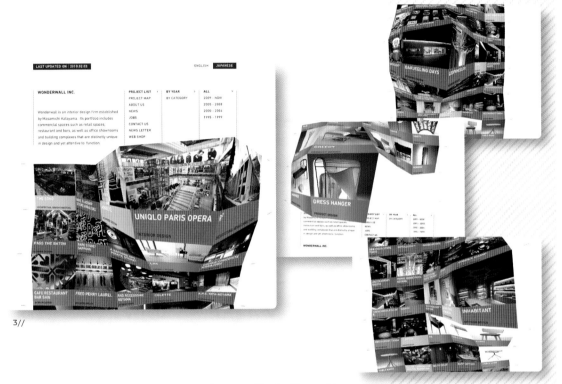

Introducing a navigation concept such as an illustration with sections of your portfolio woven into the elements of the image can be another way to heighten the overall visual experience and stand out from the crowd. Note that this approach will imply that you created the illustration, so using someone else's work in such a prominent way is not ideal.

Beware that if you aim for noticeable visual impact and the result is not executed to a high level of design quality you risk coming across as amateurish—the exact opposite of emulating the professional appearance that is important to most reviewers.

For more on specific techniques and technical information in regards to designing for visual impact, refer to Chapter Two.

1// *Serial Cut, serialcut.com* *Background imagery that stretches to all sides of the browser window frame maximizes visual impact.*

2// *Resn, resn.co.nz* *Resn's site is an intensely bizarre visual experience.*

3// *Wonderwall, wonder-wall.com* *Wonderwall's mosaic of thumbnail images stretches as you mouse over it, creating great visual impact.*

CHAPTER TWO: Implement your strategy
Consider a stopgap solution

Maybe an impending job search has got you in a hurry to get your work into a digital portfolio, or maybe you are just concerned that an all-inclusive, bells-and-whistles type of portfolio is going to take you a year to create and you want to have something in place in the meantime. It's wise to consider using one of the many free online portfolio creation and hosting services that are available to get up and running quickly, cheaply, and easily.

1//

There are other reasons to consider using an existing free service as a temporary solution: It not only provides a good dry run for preparing your portfolio content, but also gives you a clear demonstration of the qualities of industry-standard digital portfolio presentation. Well, the better ones do at least.

The services we will cover fall into three categories: professional portfolio services, social networks, and blogs. Professional portfolio services are the best for learning about the presentation style and interface elements that make up the industry standard and provide a baseline of professionalism. Social networks open up a world of online networking for gaining clients, collaborators, and admirers. Blogs can be repurposed as portfolio platforms and lend themselves to anyone interested in a digital publishing model where illustrating a history of updates is essential.

What's good for creative professionals is that there are quite a few free services to consider and you can try as many as you like. In most cases, if you like the free service and want to unlock features to take your portfolio further, you can pay a small subscription fee, which may well be worthwhile.

The six steps on pages 32–33 will guide you through creating a free online portfolio, while the reviews on pages 34–39 will help you decide which service to choose.

Quick tip

If you are considering putting a lot of time into your portfolio creation because you don't have much work to show and you want to impress reviewers with what you can do with the packaging, consider this: Put that same time into a made-up assignment and use a professional, free, off-the-shelf portfolio solution. Reviewers will appreciate seeing work that relates to the real world more than a portfolio creation assignment where you are your own client—not a very real-world scenario.

1// Marc Atlan,
krop.com/marcatlan
Compare the Krop site (top two
images) with Marc's primary custom-
built site (bottom two images) at
marcatlan.com.

Create a portfolio in six steps

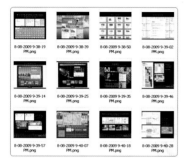

1. Prepare your work

Create digital images of the pieces you want to showcase. High-quality JPEG or PNG-24 formats work best in most cases. If your work is not digital, you will need to either photograph or scan the pieces. Take care to use professional lighting techniques and a good-quality camera. Placing the work at a slight angle relative to the camera can be an easy way to introduce some depth to your overall presentation.

2. Create a free account

Choose one of the free services outlined in this section and follow the simple steps to create your account. This can take anywhere from two to ten minutes. Free portfolio services are generally designed to be easy to use; if you encounter problems, you can always create a fresh account or move on to one of the other services.

3. Personalize

As part of your personalization, you will need to prepare your biography and resumé to include in the appropriate locations. Follow the prompts to choose the settings you desire, achieving the most personalized appearance possible. The free versions of most services offer some basic settings that allow you to modify the visual appearance of your portfolio. Usually you can choose between established templates; in some cases you can control typography and colors.

4. Upload your work

Again following the prompts, begin uploading your work piece by piece. Some of the free services limit the number of pieces you can upload. As with many other features, the limits are eased or removed altogether with the premium service, which you must pay for.

Choose and order your work carefully. Do your homework to discover what your potential employers want to see and include that. If process and thinking is important to the type of roles you seek, include sketches and sequences.

5. Annotate your work

It is important that reviewers know what your involvement in each piece was. Use the tools provided to display information about the client, the brief, your role in the project, materials or technical skills used, and any other information you feel is relevant. Be thorough but concise, remembering that employers are generally time-poor and need to get to key information quickly.

6. Review and refine

Now you have a digital portfolio, but don't stop there. Get feedback and refine your personalization, annotations, and the choices behind what pieces you're showing. A good tactic is to ask potential employers if they have any tips for your portfolio at the end of an interview. Have a thick skin and an open mind and you will gain some useful insight into how the presentation of your work is being perceived.

Free portfolio creation and hosting services

There are a number of free services available online for creating and hosting your portfolio. Here is a rundown of some of the better services out there, listed by type.

Professional portfolio services

The following are services for creating online portfolios suitable for graphic designers, illustrators, photographers, and other creative professionals. They have minimal branding and allow your identity to take center stage. In most cases you can upgrade to a subscription-based premium service for more features, personalization, and control.

Carbonmade, carbonmade.com

This is easy to use and extremely quick to set up. As far as features go, the end result is not as sophisticated as some of the others. Your "about" information is a bit hidden and you are fairly limited with the amount of detail you can display for each piece. The free service limits you to thirty-five images across five projects. You get a clean, personalized web address. If you're all about showing your designs with very little extra information, this could be the way to go.

Ease of setup and maintenance:	9/10
Professional appearance:	6/10
Personalization:	4/10
Networking exposure:	3/10
Overall rating:	6/10

deviantART's Portfolio, portfolio.deviantart.com

deviantART's Portfolio, the Awesome Version, offers a great balance of versatility, professionalism, simplicity, and usability. As with many similar services, there is a free and a premium service. One small downside is that the setup experience can be a little awkward to navigate. As a result this service may take longer to set up than some of the others and may require a bit more experience with web-based applications. Once you're through, the end result is quite professional. As a bonus, you get exposure to the entire deviantART creative network.

Ease of setup and maintenance:	6/10
Professional appearance:	9/10

Personalization: 6/10
Networking exposure: 8/10
Overall rating: 8/10

Krop Creative Database, krop.com/creativedatabase

This is a very good free service with an option to upgrade to a subscription-based version. You can create a professional-looking portfolio with biography and resumé, image browsing application, and captions. It is quick and easy to set up and gives you a good end result with a neat personalized web address. Krop positions itself as the professional service, claiming that you have enough so-called friends.

Ease of setup and maintenance: 8/10
Professional appearance: 9/10
Personalization: 7/10
Networking exposure: 4/10
Overall rating: 7/10

Cargo Collective, cargocollective.com

Possibly the best of all worlds, this service offers ease of content maintenance plus extensive personalization. There are plenty of templates to choose from as starting points, with lots of specific control beyond that. Like Tumblr (see p. 39), there's a follow feature for keeping tabs on other Cargo members. This service gets very high marks.

Ease of setup and maintenance: 9/10
Professional appearance: 9/10
Personalization: 9/10
Networking exposure: 7/10
Overall rating: 9/10

1//

2//

1// *Brianna Garcia,*
briannagarcia.daportfolio.com
Brianna's portfolio lives in a
deviantART Portfolio profile.

2// *David Arias,*
krop.com/davidarias
Krop Creative Database provides
clean, minimal, and bold templates.

Social networks

Similar to the professional portfolio services listed, these sites allow you to create a profile for free and showcase your work. The difference is that these are community-oriented sites where your own identity takes a back seat to the network's identity. There is an emphasis on collecting friends and followers in the network, and you will discover a lot of social networking features in wide use such as the ability for others to leave comments about your work. This approach may or may not be appropriate for you. It can come across as less professional in a traditional sense, but has other benefits including networking, ideas and information sharing, and visibility with potential employers.

The Behance Network, behance.net

Signing up to the Behance Network gives you a free portfolio with standard features but very little presentation customization. You automatically appear in the network where other creative people can find and follow you, and prospective employers can review your work. The portfolio format consists of a gallery-style main interface with scrolling pages for detail when reviewers drill down. It supports images and video uploads. They have put some thoughtful details into the fairly advanced administrative side, such as a quick tutorial to view before you use the content editor.

Ease of setup and maintenance:	7/10
Professional appearance:	7/10
Personalization:	7/10
Networking exposure:	9/10
Overall rating:	8/10

Coroflot, coroflot.com

Coroflot offers a good, clean interface with a prominent but not overstated location for your biography. As it's still about the community, your identity takes a little bit of a back seat to Coroflot's, but you gain the benefits of being part of a creative community.

Ease of setup and maintenance:	7/10
Professional appearance:	7/10
Personalization:	7/10
Networking exposure:	7/10
Overall rating:	7/10

deviantART, deviantART.com

One of the most popular creative social networking sites, deviantART is a bustling hive of all kinds of creative energy. At times it can border on the MySpace style of experience, which might not be the professional look you want. Flashing banner ads don't help either. Is this a fun and rewarding experience for the right people? Absolutely. Is it a viable option for a professional-looking portfolio? Probably not. Best to check out the professional portfolio tool that deviantART created for that.

Ease of setup and maintenance:	6/10
Professional appearance:	1/10
Personalization:	4/10
Networking exposure:	7/10
Overall rating:	4/10

Flickr, flickr.com

This is arguably one of the most popular creativity-oriented social networks of all time. Intended to be primarily a photo organization and sharing platform, it can be used to host a digital portfolio very easily. This can be an appropriate option if you would like to engage in an active, positive, creative community. Your identity will take a back seat to the network's. To certain reviewers it may appear a cheap option. However, if you put the effort into getting the right views of your work in there with the right amount of information about your skills and roles, it can be an effective platform.

1// *Mike Chan, behance.net/mike7*
A popular portfolio on Behance.

Ease of setup and maintenance:	7/10
Professional appearance:	6/10
Personalization:	2/10
Networking exposure:	8/10
Overall rating:	6/10

2// *Adam Mulyadi,*
coroflot.com/public/individual_details.
asp?individual_id=282174
Coroflot provides a simple,
clean interface.

1//

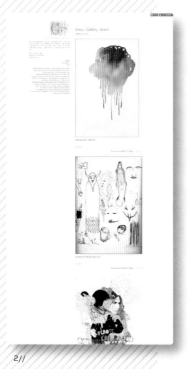

2//

RedBubble, redbubble.com

RedBubble is an arts-and-crafts kind of community with a powerful e-commerce angle. Best suited to artists, illustrators, and photographers in many ways, the service gives you a shop front that operates something like a stand at a local arts market. Visitors can browse your work and then purchase framed prints, T-shirts, posters, and other products featuring your work from you while RedBubble handles the fulfillment.

Ease of setup and maintenance:	7/10
Professional appearance:	6/10
Personalization:	5/10
Networking exposure:	7/10
Overall rating:	6/10

Blogs

Free blogging services can be repurposed as an online portfolio. The benefit is that you can add as much extra information as you like. This is a suitable solution if you plan on making updates frequently and have a lot to say. Active blogging can help with search engine page ranking and with raising your digital profile in general. Blogs by default provide an auto-archiving main view with detail views for each blog post. You can choose to add each individual piece of work as a separate blog post or add them in groups based on projects or types. Blog platforms support images, text, and embedded video.

Blogger, blogger.com

This popular, Google-owned free blogging service allows anyone to create a new blog in minutes and start uploading images and text straight away. Choose from a handful of templates to control the appearance. The administrative options do not seem as powerful as that of rival WordPress.

Ease of setup and maintenance:	6/10
Professional appearance:	4/10
Personalization:	5/10
Networking exposure:	8/10
Overall rating:	6/10

Tumblr, tumblr.com

Tumblr's simplicity is one of its best assets. It lets you post anything and you can customize nearly every aspect of your presentation. It has been described as microblogging in its purest form—after Twitter, of course. Approached in the right way and for the right audience, it can work as a digital portfolio.

Ease of setup and maintenance:	7/10
Professional appearance:	6/10
Personalization:	7/10
Networking exposure:	6/10
Overall rating:	6/10

WordPress, wordpress.com

This is another popular free blog platform with a powerful administrative interface. Choose from a wide variety of visual and structural templates and create multiple pages along with categories for your blog posts.

Ease of setup and maintenance:	6/10
Professional appearance:	6/10
Personalization:	6/10
Networking exposure:	7/10
Overall rating:	6/10

Quick tip

For quick and easy blog posting to more than one blog at a time, download a blogging tool and you will be able to post without having to visit your blog host to log in.

PC users can use Windows' free software Live Writer. It allows you to paste images directly from any image-editing tool and accepts most common embedded video players. Download Windows Live Writer at download.live.com/writer.

Mac users can use Blogo, available from drinkbrainjuice.com/blogo.

1// Bonnie Jones,
bonniejonesphoto.wordpress.com

2// Gabrielle Rose,
drawgabbydraw.tumblr.com

The main content framework categories

When you factor in all the variables you can adjust to create the perfect portfolio to suit your needs, there are an infinite number of possible outcomes. It is useful when planning the content structure that will work best for you to consider the four main framework categories: gallery view, single scrolling page (vertical or horizontal), list navigation, and conceptual.

Note that elements of these types can be combined to create hybrids. In fact, most well-designed portfolios are combinations of more than one type. There are many examples of portfolios that at first glance appear to be completely unique, but the underlying structure may be entirely traditional. The use of these familiar structures can mean that your visitors are more likely to connect intuitively with the presentation of your work.

1//

2//

1. Gallery view

Perhaps the most common type of portfolio structure, the gallery view begins with a main view that has thumbnails representing individual pieces or projects. Reviewers can drill down into each item to see a detailed view or views, along with more information about your involvement in the work.

A common addition to the gallery view is a lightbox feature for viewing the detail of your pieces with minimal other information on the page. This is best when combined with slideshow forward and back controls.

A current trend is to take advantage of today's larger screen areas by having oversized thumbnails. Use of these can mean that visitors get a good sense of the nature of the work being presented even before they drill down into detail.

When preparing thumbnail images for use in a gallery view, consider rules of good composition and avoid scaling work down to such a size that the content is indistinguishable. A thumbnail does not need to be literally a scaled-down version of the detail view. It can instead be a cropped closeup of a particularly interesting aspect of the work being shown.

When executed well, the gallery view provides a good balance between a professional, easy-to-use presentation, and something that is scalable, flexible, and relatively easy to maintain.

3//

1// Kidplastik, Drew Taylor,
kidplastik.com
A thumbnail-based gallery format.

2// Hello Monday,
hellomonday.net
This site combines a gallery view with
an expand–collapse detail view.

3// Marumiyan, marumiyan.com
A mosaic approach to the gallery
format can suit bold and colorful work.

2. Scrolling view

A somewhat simpler option is to take advantage of the browser scrollbars. As long as the work is clearly displayed, there is nothing terribly wrong with a long scrolling page for displaying content. The benefit is that this is very easy to implement and simple for reviewers to navigate. The vertical scrolling view is the native format for blogs.

To view the detail of any given piece or project, a similar approach can be taken as with the gallery view—reviewers can drill down to see more screens from that project, view more information about your involvement, and what the work was for.

2//

There is a myth in web design circles that people don't find content that's "below the fold" (below the area visible without scrolling). User testing has shown that many of us are now quite used to using the scrollbar almost immediately and even referring to it with a quick glance to check the size of the bar as an indicator of the length of the page.

One mistake to avoid is to design the page in such a way that the fold falls in a large gap in content so that the page appears to end. This can create the perception that there's nothing to scroll to. Better practice is to design for the fold to be cutting some content in half so it becomes obvious that there is more content below.

Design tip

Remember that people are more accustomed to a vertical scrolling page than a horizontal one; if you choose horizontal you may need to call visitors' attention to the horizontal scrolling structure.

In general, horizontal scrolling can be a bit awkward and less intuitive than vertical scrolling. If you choose this option, proceed with caution; consider building a quick prototype so that you can observe people using it and check whether they encounter any problems.

1// Michael Kleinman,
samegoes.com
Vertical scrolling view.

2// Joe Bauldoff, bauldoff.com
Horizontal scrolling view.

3. List navigation

This type uses a written list of projects or sections as a persistent navigation element for moving through your portfolio. Often displayed on the left-hand side, the list is clickable and allows reviewers to jump from one project or area of the site to another without having to return to the main page.

A variation on the list navigation is the use of a collapsing and expanding mechanism for an accordion-like effect. Project names can be rolled up into categories. Clicking a category will cause that section to expand to reveal the projects in the list that fit into that category without changing the display of content in the main body of the page until an actual project has been clicked. This can be handy if you have a large amount of work across many categories.

One disadvantage of the list navigation approach is the lack of room to display thumbnail images of the projects. This can be overcome, however, by combining this structure type with the front-page style of the gallery type. This results in a more visual first impression.

1//

2//

If you have a strong typographic sense, designing a custom list navigation element can be a good way to offset your visuals.

When tackling navigation design—which is discussed in greater detail later in this chapter—it becomes important to create a system that tells people where they are in the site at any given time. By highlighting the project being viewed we give the reviewer orientation and therefore provide a smoother, more intuitive, experience.

1// Face, designbyface.com;
code by Modulor, modulorweb.com
Expand–collapse mechanism with
prominent typography.

2// Michele Angelo,
superexpresso.com
An example of a list navigation
system with "new" markers
indicating the latest content.

4. Conceptual

This is a broad category and can be more challenging to execute well. When handled poorly it can appear to be pitching the portfolio itself rather than your work, and can result in usability issues.

To pull this type off you need a great concept and quite often a visual metaphor to provide a unique navigation system for reviewers to explore your work. This structure can often be the least scalable of the four types, as adding a new section to your portfolio can leave you going back to the drawing board.

When well executed, the conceptual content framework can be a surefire way to stand out from the crowd. Refer to later in this chapter for notes on getting a bit more creative.

In summary: When getting started on sketching your portfolio structure, consider these four frameworks and mix and match the features of each to develop the structure that is ideal for you. There are strengths, weaknesses, challenges, and opportunities with each.

1//

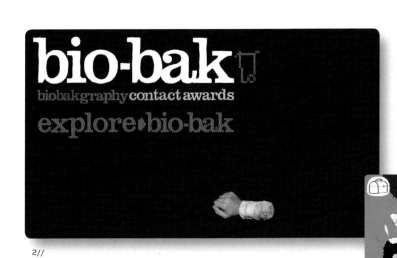

2//

Here's an indicative ranking of the four main types by three key values:

Scalability:
1. Gallery view
2. List navigation
3. Scrolling page
4. Conceptual

Originality:
1. Conceptual
2. List navigation
3. Scrolling page
4. Gallery view

Professionalism:
1. Gallery view
2. List navigation
3. Scrolling page
4. Conceptual

1// Chuck U, chucku.com
Framework and content become one in this example of an illustration-based navigation system.

2// Bio-bak, bio-bak.nl
This site turns navigation into a game—a gutsy but impressive tactic.

Information architecture

The information architecture of your portfolio is a bit like a skeleton—it is the underlying structure that holds everything together. Getting it right is both an art and a science, as it involves the organizing and labeling of elements to contribute to the overall usability of the site.

Your decisions about what content you group together in what parts of your site and what you call those groupings are more important than you might think. Consider the following:

Joe Illustrator wants to include pieces spanning a number of years and many project types. He plans for an area of his site to be called "Illustration," but when he dumps all of his work in one big section, he winds up with some fairly out-there older work next to some recent corporate pieces in a way that is jarring. In the end he settles on multiple subsections within Illustration: Posters, Editorial, Corporate, and Older Work. This way he knows future corporate clients won't be thrown off by his early personal work.

Decisions such as these regarding the naming and grouping of pieces of content in your site will greatly affect the overall experience a visitor has. This effort is information architecture.

If you are looking for the most direct path to clear and intuitive high-level architecture for a standard portfolio site, look no further than:

Portfolio

About

Contact

If you have a lot of work across a number of projects that demonstrates abilities across multiple disciplines, your architecture could look more like this:

Portfolio
   Illustration
      Editorial
      Publishing
      Posters
      Album Covers
      Personal
   Graphic Design
      Book Covers
      Album Covers
      Websites
      Personal
   Photography
      Landscapes
      People
      Journalism
      Personal
About
Contact

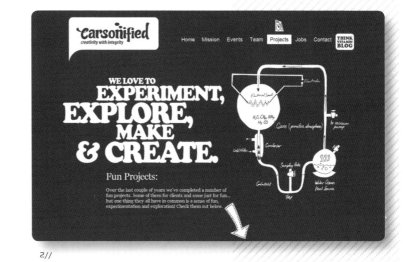

2//

Consider that the length of a list of options is directly linked to the findability of things. Each list, depending on the way it is presented, has an optimal length beyond which it becomes irritatingly too full of options. Breaking longer lists into subcategories, as in the above example, makes the overall structure more easily scannable and provides a better experience.

1// Marumiyan,
marumiyan.com
An example of an intuitive
architecture clearly displayed using
an indented list navigation system.

2// Carsonified,
carsonified.com
The Carsonified site is well structured
and easy to interpret at a glance.

49

Navigation design

Once you have determined your information architecture, you can begin work on what type of navigation system best suits your purposes. The most standard approaches involve placing the names of your main sections in a row along the top of each page beneath the identity of the site, or along the left-hand side of each page. Beyond this, there are an infinite number of variations, both straightforward and highly conceptual.

A common practice in navigation design for sites that contain a large amount of information is to list the subsections of each main section in a drop-down menu that appears when someone rolls their cursor over the navigation. Not only does this provide quick access to all parts of the site, it also gives an indication of the site's structure at a glance without needing to leave the page.

It is a good idea to have navigation elements change appearance when the cursor rolls over them. This simple gesture acts like a beckoning hand as if to say, yes, there's good content this way, so go ahead and click.

To help orient people as they move through your site, it is best to design your navigation in such a way that their current location is indicated. This can be done visually by highlighting the current page in the navigation.

When exploring ways to take navigation design further, consider putting imagery, animation, or video in panels that appear when the cursor rolls over the navigation to help entice a click by way of describing the contents of each section.

1//   2//

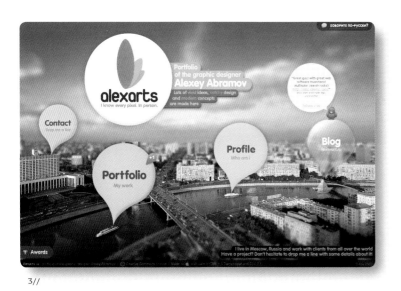

3//

If you are creating a highly conceptual or visually theme-based portfolio, think of ways to integrate your navigation design into your chosen direction: It is a key functional element of the site and a core part of the overall interactivity. Explore ways to tie the navigation design into your central idea via a visual metaphor if appropriate. Remember not to sacrifice usability, however.

A good navigation system needs to be entirely usable and intuitive. If it is not, the resulting experience will annoy people and reflect badly on you.

Be sure to make the target areas large enough that they are easy to click. If the elements in your navigation are so small that someone has to focus to put the cursor exactly in the right spot, you have created a potentially annoying usability issue. On a related note, make sure the text in your navigation system is legible, for obvious reasons.

1// Kareem King,
kx2web.com
An example of an entire navigation system contained in one pull-down menu—clean and simple.

2// Darek Nyckowiak,
thetoke.com
3D panels to flip through by way of a horizontal slider make a slick navigation device.

3// Alexey Abramov,
alexarts.ru
Presenting navigation choices in the context of content on your homepage can make for a well-integrated experience.

Descriptions display

The design that you apply to the descriptions of your work falls into the realm of information design. Come up short in this area and the experience of browsing your work can become confusing and muddled. Get it right and you can achieve a seamless presentation where the viewer's eye will always find a rewarding place to land as they look for the answers to questions such as, "This appears to be a collaborative piece—what was this person's role?"; "What was the brief on this project?"; and "Did this project achieve the desired results for the client?" As established in Chapter One, it is a good idea to convey some combination of the project title, the client name, your role, and any other key information depending on the nature of your work. Other considerations to bear in mind include:

- Keep the information as concise as possible.
- Position the information in a consistent location for each piece so reviewers don't need to hunt high and low to find it each time.
- Use clear and legible typography unless you have a very solid conceptual reason for deviating. Even then, think again.
- Proof your text thoroughly to make sure there are no mistakes. Typos do no one any favors.

Ninety percent of good information design involves knowing the optimal underlying hierarchy to use with the content that you are displaying. The number-one priority should be the project title. When structured properly, this single piece of information will get the reviewer a large portion of the way toward understanding what they are looking at and what you had to do with it.

1//

2//

3//

Examples of good project naming structure:

- Album cover illustration
- Cosmetics packaging design
- Poster design for theatrical performance

Why is the title worth focusing on? Because with the right
structure you can explain:

1. What it is your visitors are looking at ("poster")
2. The key discipline that you employed on the job ("design")
3. What subject matter area the project lives in
   ("theatrical performance" = "entertainment industry").

This tells us we should structure our titles thoughtfully and
make them visually prominent. A useful analogy to consider
in the design of your descriptions display is the small placards
you find next to paintings in an art gallery. They are treated
consistently, are concise and informative, but never risk
upstaging the actual work.

1// JPEG Interactive,
jpeg.cn
*Data visualization is used effectively
by JPEG Interactive to make
a sophisticated-looking and
informative interface.*

2// Juan Diego Velasco,
juandiegovelasco.com
*Clean, consistent, and simple, these
descriptions are easily scanned and
quickly convey a breadth of skills.*

3// Hello Monday,
hellomonday.net
*Examples of clearly displayed project
titles and descriptive overviews used
consistently across all projects.*

Screen area optimization

The majority of people browsing the web are looking at websites through the dimensions of 1024 pixels wide x 768 pixels high. Following close on the heels of that in most statistical snapshots is 1280 x 800 and 1280 x 1024. Given that your target audience will often be other creative professionals, we can assume that fairly large screen areas will be prevalent among those viewing your site.

Your site will be viewed by a wide range of devices and configurations, so it is important to revisit the strategy formed in the first chapter and consider the appropriate tactics. Are you targeting creative professionals? If yes, go for layouts optimized for 1280-pixel-wide displays and make the most of the available area. Generally speaking, horizontal scrollbars are undesirable (unless they are a key feature in your site's navigation; see pages 42–43), so look at ways to have visual impact across 1280 pixels but with important foreground content sitting within 1024.

1//

The page "fold" is the imaginary line below which a viewer must scroll in order to see the content. Putting content below the fold on a 1024 x 768 display is not a problem, but you should make sure the content that sits above the fold is compelling enough and arranged in such a way that visitors are enticed to scroll down.

Some additional guidelines to consider:

Avoid putting your work in a small box in the middle of the screen as if you are optimizing for 800 x 600: these screen dimensions are now almost completely obsolete.

2//

3//

Design tip

If your strategy dictates that your portfolio should work well on mobile devices, you will need to think things through from a number of different angles, some technical and some design-oriented. The working prototype stage is a good time to try viewing the site on devices such as an iPhone. You will get a sense for what works and what doesn't.

Invent ways to have background imagery that flows beyond the borders of 1024 x 768 so those viewing through larger dimensions continue to have a visually rich experience. View your site on displays of different dimensions so you are aware of how different it can look on different devices.

Think about the difference between centering your layouts as opposed to having them left- or right-aligned. In most cases, center alignment is the most flattering, as it helps to avoid accidental-looking negative space. Will your site be fixed-width or variable (will it stay the same width or will it change as a viewer changes their browser window dimensions)? If variable, there will always be a minimum width—what will yours be? What's the ideal scenario that many web designers strive to achieve?

- Variable or fixed width depending on the execution
- Center-aligned
- Looks great on 1024 x 768 with no horizontal scrollbar
- Looks amazing on 1280 x 1024

1// *magneticNorth (mN),*
mnatwork.com
Visitors draw shapes to reveal content
using the entire screen area.

2// *Mika Mäkinen, mcinen.net*
Mika Mäkinen uses Flash to create a
full window background effect.

3// *Justin Maller, justinmaller.com*
A mosaic of large-scale thumbnails
maximizes visual impact.

Usability

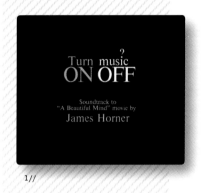

1//

2//

Good usability in web design means reducing the number of questions in the minds of your site's visitors as they move from page to page. Good usability is the baseline expectation of a professional portfolio site. Introduce bad usability and you will damage your image.

Is your site's navigation easy to find, read, understand, and click? It is easy to let your typographic sense and the use of scale contrast get the better of you when designing your site's navigation. That intricate typeface that looks incredible at 76pt 300dpi print may not translate to 12pt 72dpi. Aim for ease of navigation through your pages or risk irritating your viewers.

Does your site design do a good job of telling people where they are? The use of a clear identity for yourself (most likely your name) placed prominently and consistently throughout the site, plus page headings and a navigation system that indicates where you are in the site, are some useful ways to orientate people. Location awareness is important because it helps with overall findability and time slicing (explained below).

Knowing where you are helps you get from points A to B. Page titles that appear in bookmarks and at the top of the browser window help with location awareness on other levels. Time slicing is when we give visitors enough information so they can guess how long they will need to view your site or sections of it. Tools such as "1 of 10" when viewing multiple detail views strung together help achieve this.

Is the information about you and your work clearly and legibly presented? Consider the level of contrast between page background and foreground text. Cascading Style Sheets (CSS), which determine the visual style of your site in conjunction with XHTML (to be discussed in greater detail later in this chapter), allow you to control line height as well. The distance between lines of text in a paragraph can greatly affect legibility.

Another common technique for improving readability in body text is to keep the text column width from stretching much beyond 75 characters. There is some evidence to support that optimal line length is a myth, however. Explore the debate on the web and decide for yourself.

Other tips to consider:

Launch PDF documents in a new window, as they disrupt the normal flow of navigation between HTML pages and should be kept separate.

Avoid methods of launching popup windows with JavaScript that get blocked by popup blockers such as Google Toolbar.

Avoid having elements on your pages that look as if they should be clickable not be linked anywhere. If something looks as if you could click it (thumbnail images, for example), link it to the most predictable place for it to lead.

Quick tip

Always link your logo or name back to the homepage. This is standard across most sites and people have come to expect it.

1// Oleg Kostuk,
theoleg.com
Music that plays automatically can annoy some people. The Oleg asks our preference at the front door.

2// Rob Palmer,
branded07.com
An example of clear and easy-to-use navigation.

3// squareFACTOR,
squarefuctor.com
This site offers helpful signposting and navigation controls throughout the experience.

3//

XHTML, CSS, and JavaScript

1//

2//

1// What web pages look like
beneath the surface.

2// Adobe Dreamweaver.

3// The Norik, thenorik.com
A portfolio built in Indexhibit.

If you are reading this page you may be interested in creating your portfolio pages from scratch. We will cover some basic definitions and a high-level overview. Note that there is a wealth of information and resources on these topics on the web, and there is no limit to how far you can take your technical skills if so inclined. Prepare for acronym overload as we dive into the realm of Presentation Layer Development (PLD).

Extensible Hypertext Markup Language (XHTML) is the framework and content of the pages of your web-based portfolio. It is what web browsers such as Internet Explorer, Firefox, Safari, and Chrome read in order to know what to display back to you on each page. For most basic portfolio sites this is where your content will live (your text and image references).

Cascading Style Sheets (CSS) determine the visual style and layout of the content and structure of your pages. CSS enables the appearance of your pages to be kept separate from the content, such that you can modify your style sheet and change the look of all your pages at once.

JavaScript is a scripting language that can be used for additional features and effects that plain XHTML and CSS can't achieve.

If you want to see what all of this looks like under the surface, choose to "view source" in your web browser while viewing a web page and you'll get a view of raw XHTML and possibly JavaScript. The CSS code often lives in a separate file, although it can be placed inline.

How do you go about creating your own XHTML, CSS, and JavaScript? Essentially there are three approaches: Hand coding; use of a WYSIWYG (What You See Is What You Get) editor; or a combination of the two.

Hand coding requires that you learn the tags that comprise XHTML and the rules used in CSS and write them via a basic text editor (or specialized coding software) line by line. It can be tedious to learn and create. Most designers who create their own pages use a WYSIWYG and jump into hand coding as needed.

A WYSIWYG editor is a program that works like a basic text editor such as Microsoft Word, but it saves to XHTML and CSS files. It lets you create layouts, visual styles, and content with an intuitive interface that provides a preview as you go. Most WYSIWYGs worth their salt let you jump back and forth between the default editing mode and hand coding.

Adobe Creative Suite includes Dreamweaver, which is an excellent tool for creating your own pages. If you design your pages in Photoshop, there is the means to automatically output basic HTML directly from your Photoshop files and then open them in Dreamweaver to refine and apply further development.

Tech tip

A free application that is increasingly popular with creative professionals can be downloaded at indexhibit.org. In their own words, it is "A web application used to build and maintain an archetypal, invisible website format that combines text, image, movie and sound."

Some basic knowledge of web development is helpful in setting up an Indexhibit site. You will still need your own web hosting, but the end result is a very flexible platform with easy-to-use content-maintenance tools.

The forum gives helpful advice on all kinds of web development issues relating to presenting creative work online: indexhibit.org/forum.

3//

Working with Flash

Adobe Flash is an amazing tool for bringing interactive motion and lively animation into your portfolio. Over the years it has evolved from its origins as a vector and timeline-based animation tool to a robust platform supporting bitmap graphics, video, dynamic content, and more.

Like any advanced tool, in the wrong hands Flash can be used to commit great sins of bad taste. If you choose to experiment, make sure you objectively evaluate what you are creating as you go so you don't fall into the trap of being mesmerized by basic techniques. Putting flashy animation and cheap effects into your portfolio presentation without purpose can reflect badly on your image.

1//

Only Flash-enabled browsers can view Flash files, although there are ways of using JavaScript to display alternate content for non-Flash browsers. However, according to most indicative statistics sources, the vast majority of visitors to your site will have Flash-enabled browsers.

One of the drawbacks of Flash is the likelihood of decreased Search Engine Optimization (SEO). When text is embedded in Flash, search engines can't get to it as easily. There are ways around this, and advances in technology mean that this area is improving, but in general if you need good page ranking in search engines avoid putting all your content in Flash. If your entire portfolio lives in one Flash file, you lose the ability to have unique web addresses for different parts of your site. There are ways around this using advanced Flash Action Script development.

2//

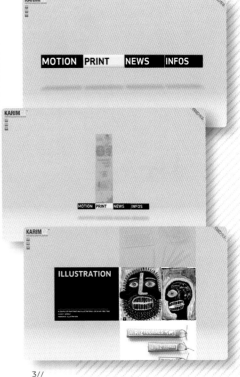
3//

To avoid these pitfalls, consider creating a site with content mainly in plain HTML but with individual Flash files embedded in the pages to create movement and visual interest.

If you are really game (or can partner with a Flash developer colleague), you can work up ways to integrate a concept into a fully interactive and animated experience using Flash. There really is no limit to what you can achieve with the right talent. The ability to display video effectively blows the doors wide open, as tools such as Adobe After Effects can be used to create motion-graphics effects output to video to be delivered in Flash as FLV files.

To view and interact with a huge library of amazing Flash sites, visit the popular online showcase The FWA: Favourite Website Awards at thefwa.com.

1// *Oleg Kostuk, theoleg.com*
This creative has used Flash to design
an immersive storytelling experience.

2// *Nick Jones, narrowdesign.com*
A clean, attractive, and intuitive
Flash interface.

3// *Karim Charlebois-Zariffa,*
karimzariffa.com; site built in Flash
by Philippe Roy, unldeuxp.com
Flash is used in this portfolio to
create a great sense of depth.

Video players and lightbox displays

Embedding video in any site is easy thanks to services like Vimeo and, of course, YouTube. In terms of presentation style, a branded video player may not be exactly what you had in mind.

If you have seen what an embedded Vimeo player looks like in a web page and are happy with this presentation style, simply create your free account at vimeo.com and follow the prompts to upload your content. Grab the embed code and place it in your XHTML files placed where you want the video to appear.

For a non-branded player, convert your video files to FLV format and display them by way of a Flash video player embedded in your XHTML pages. This method gives you all the presentation control of Flash and a video platform that allows anyone with a Flash-enabled browser to view your content.

The player comes with standard controls that are designed to a decent visual and usability standard and work well. To take things further, you can customize the appearance of the controls with the expertise of a Flash developer. Note that implementing your own Flash video player requires fairly advanced knowledge of Flash development.

Alternatively, download a standalone FLV player such as the MAXI Player available from flvplayer. net/players/maxi. Use the instructions there and from what you can find on the web to implement it.

1//

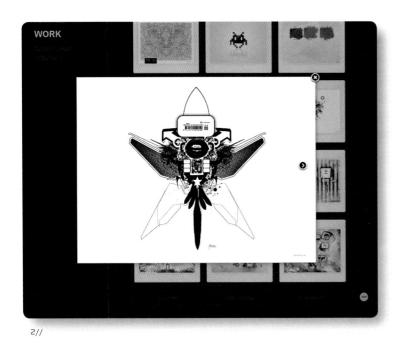

2//

A lightbox display is a viewing mode characterized by the presentation of a single enlarged image laid over the top of the page from which that enlargement was accessed. The original page gets darkened, which causes the enlargement in the foreground to stand out. Typically there are controls for moving forward and backward through other enlarged views and a close button for returning to the original page.

The benefit of a lightbox display is that it provides focus for reviewers when you want them to zero in on a particular image. To implement a lightbox display in a site you have built yourself, investigate some of the free JavaScript and jQuery solutions available on the web by searching "lightbox." In most cases, a working knowledge of JavaScript is helpful in implementing a lightbox display in this manner.

1// *Embeddable creative process video from MIND Castle on Vimeo, vimeo.com/8362481.*

2// *Lightbox display on the portfolio site of Alexey Chenishov, ftdesigner.net.*

Collaborating with a developer

Especially for students, collaborating with your peers can be a great way to obtain valuable solutions without paying full professional rates. The most common scenario may involve two students getting ready to launch their careers, one a designer and one a web developer. The designer designs both of their portfolio sites and the developer develops both of their sites.

If your portfolio is handcrafted, reviewers may be keen to know what aspect of the finished product you actually took care of. Be prepared to answer questions on this, especially if your portfolio packaging is particularly interesting or off the beaten track. If you have collaborated with a colleague, you should consider giving them a credit in the footer of each page, such as "Site built by xxxx," with a link to their own site. If you have entered into a barter arrangement then naturally they could reciprocate with a link on their site back to yours. Partnerships such as these can be helpful down the track for generating business leads by referral.

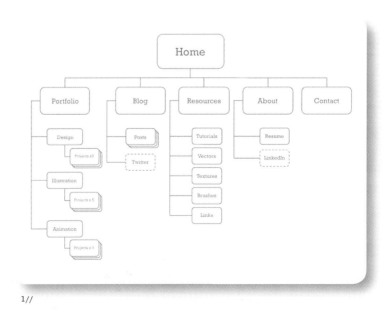

1//

Some basic things to keep in mind when collaborating with others:

1. Clear communication is essential to any collaboration.
2. Mutual respect for each other's time and opinions will go a long way toward the success of the project.
3. Brainstorm as a team and you'll be surprised at the creativity and design insight lurking in the minds of some developers. When it comes time to roll up your sleeves, clearly specify what you're looking for the developer to build. Provide helpful documents such as a site map diagram, wireframes indicating what content goes on what pages, and clean, well-labeled Photoshop documents indicating the visual design you need them to build. It's a good idea to provide JPEG previews of the mockups as well for reference. Remember that in most cases they will need the font software you used in your designs for outputting graphics.
4. It's good to agree to a deadline for any collaborative project to help with setting milestones and prioritization. If you don't, it's too easy for both of you to let the project slip indefinitely.

It is important for designers to remember that it's easier to change a Photoshop mockup in most cases than it is to redevelop a page that has already been built, so be mindful of the developer's time and energy and work toward a clear and well-thought-out specification of what they are building before they begin.

2//

1// Typically referred to as a site map, a view such as this can serve as a high-level blueprint for your site.

2// Wireframes give an indication of approximate content distribution and overall site functionality. These examples are considered "low fidelity"—they have very little detail.

Crowdsourcing

Crowdsourcing is the act of outsourcing a task, such as the development of your portfolio site, to a group or "crowd" of people. There are sites out there that enable this. Here's how it works:

1. Visit a crowdsourcing service that caters to web development, such as TopCoder Direct (topcoder.com/direct).
2. Register for an account.
3. Use the site navigation to make your way to launching a project. You may be looking to launch a "UI prototype" project in the context of the wide spectrum of types of development projects.
4. Follow the steps to create a project based on the designed "storyboard" you will have already created for your site.
5. Once you activate your project, developers will have the ability to compete to create a prototype of your site to your specification. You will choose a winner and pay that individual for their service.

That's the basic overview. There's a lot of detail on the topic to be absorbed if you choose to go down this path. It's a good idea to do some research and read what people have to say about the entire process; it has created quite a lot of discussion.

1//

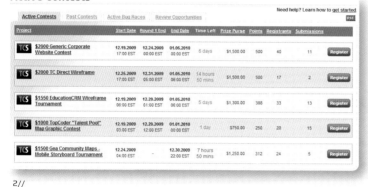

Active Contests

Need help? Learn how to get started

Active Contests	Past Contests	Active Bug Races	Review Opportunities						RSS

Project	Start Date	Round 1 End	End Date	Time Left	Prize Purse	Points	Registrants	Submissions	
TCS $2000 Generic Corporate Website Contest	12.19.2009 17:00 EST	12.24.2009 00:00 EST	01.06.2010 00:00 EST	6 days	$1,500.00	500	40	11	Register
TCS $2000 TC Direct Wireframe	12.25.2009 17:00 EST	12.31.2009 05:00 EST	01.05.2010 06:00 EST	14 hours 50 mins	$1,500.00	500	17	2	Register
TCS $1550 EducationCRM Wireframe Tournament	12.19.2009 06:00 EST	12.29.2009 01:00 EST	01.05.2010 06:00 EST	5 days	$1,300.00	388	33	13	Register
TCS $1000 TopCoder "Talent Pool" Map Graphic Contest	12.19.2009 03:00 EST	12.29.2009 12:00 EST	01.01.2010 00:00 EST	1 day	$750.00	250	20	15	Register
TCS $1500 Gea Community Maps - Mobile Storyboard Tournament	12.24.2009 04:00 EST	-	12.30.2009 22:00 EST	7 hours 50 mins	$1,250.00	312	24	5	Register

2//

To crowdsource or not to crowdsource? Some pros and cons:

Pros
1. You only pay for a successfully developed site that you are happy with, so there is less risk of hiring someone, not getting what you want, and still having to pay them.
2. Developers will compete for your project.
3. You can get good value for money.

Cons
1. It can be difficult to maintain a good working relationship with crowdsourced developers throughout the life of the project.
2. You may not get the solution you were looking for and may be looking at additional costs to get there.
3. There can be increased chances that the project fails due to issues such as lack of high pay, the remoteness of the developer, and the risk of having too few competing developers.

Crowdsourcing in general is a controversial topic. Before you participate on either side of a contest, read up on the debate in order to make informed choices about your participation.

1// TopCoder Direct,

topcoder.com/direct

TopCoder is a crowdsourcing

community for developers

and designers.

2// TopCoder Studio,

topcoder.com/studio

Example of a list of "contests" in

which developers may compete.

Web hosting

In order for your collection of XHTML files, CSS files, Flash files, and images to form a publicly available website, they need to sit on a fully functioning web server. Luckily this is an easily accessed service provided by many companies.

There are several features and pricing options to consider when shopping for the right web hosting solution. A general rule with hosting costs is that the higher the volume of traffic the site gets, the higher the cost of hosting. For most portfolio sites, especially when you're just starting out, we'll assume fairly low traffic.

Shared hosting, as opposed to dedicated servers that large web-based businesses rely on, is adequate for a portfolio site. Shared hosting gives you access to an administrative control panel and FTP access for uploading files to your site.

Other common features and specifications include the following approximations:

- 10GB to 100GB of storage
- 100MB to 1TB of bandwidth
- Allowance for hosting multiple domains
- Up to 1000 individual email accounts
- Web-based access to your email
- A database platform
- Analytics for viewing your traffic statistics

The cheapest but still reliable hosting options are often offered by US-based providers. You can find hosting for less than US$5 per month. Some providers offer cheaper rates if you commit to a longer-term contract. Consider going with an established provider, as they tend to know what they're doing and offer better customer support.

Here's a short list of reputable providers:

- Media Temple: mediatemple.net
- Godaddy: godaddy.com
- Rackspace: rackspace.com and rackspace.co.uk

For more providers and other resources, visit *clazie.com/ digitalportfolios.*

A useful feature offered by some providers such as Media Temple is one-click installation of popular services such as WordPress blogs. This comes in handy if you want to add features to your site without the extra development time to install them by hand.

Cloud hosting is a slightly more expensive option that provides more hosting resources in the event that something on your site becomes very popular overnight. If the extra resources are called on, you will get charged for it.

There is such a thing as free web hosting; providers offer free hosting in exchange for displaying a link or banner on your site.

You can obtain a personalized web address by registering a domain name if it is available through a hosting provider. You will need to pay for the use of the name for as long as you plan to have it. Your hosting provider will associate this name with your portfolio and email addresses.

Tech tip

If you plan to do more than host XHTML, CSS, Flash, and images on your site, consider what your backend programming will mean for your hosting requirements. For example, applications developed in .Net require Windows hosting, whereas PHP applications should be hosted on Linux.

1//

1// Media Temple's control panel.

Revisit your strategy

If the creative process is like a rocket launcher, you want to be sure you're pointing it in the right direction, so revisit your strategy before you prepare to come up with something unique and inspired.

What are you trying to achieve? Be specific when you answer this. Don't just say to yourself that you want to get work. What kind of work do you want? With what type of employer or client? Found and hired by what type of professional? Ultimately respected and admired by what type of peers?

For example, your answers might run along the lines of:

Q: What am I trying to achieve by having this online portfolio?
A: To attract and engage potential clients and build my personal brand.

Q: What kind of work do I want?
A: Freelance advertising creative and art direction.

Q: With what type of employer or client?
A: Above the line advertising agencies.

Q: Found and hired by what type of professional?
A: Leading creative directors.

Q: Ultimately respected and admired by what type of peers?
A: Other creatives and art directors, creative directors, and clients.

These answers point to the need to communicate your ability to create things that elicit an emotional response. You will also need to provide a clear indication of your experience working from challenging commercially driven advertising briefs. Possible tactical solution: Devise a challenging commercially driven brief for yourself and come up with an innovative portfolio presentation solution to answer it.

If your answers indicate that you are aiming for a broad appeal to a wide audience across a range of skills, you'll want to bear this in mind when refining the ideas that stem from your brainstorming. The more you expect of your portfolio in terms of messaging and target audience, the more challenging it can be to integrate innovative concepts. The wider your scope the more important aspects such as usability and ease of navigation become.

Answers that indicate the need for a broad appeal approach could be:

Q: What am I trying to achieve by having this online portfolio?
A: To attract freelance clients across multiple types of creative services and potentially a long-term position at a creativity-centered company.

Q: What kind of work do I want?
A: Freelance illustration, photography, and graphic design.

Q: With what type of employer or client?
A: Boutique creative agencies and direct clients.

Q: Found and hired by what type of professional?
A: Creative directors, marketing directors, anyone and everyone.

Q: Ultimately respected and admired by what type of peers?
A: Designers, illustrators, photographers, creative directors, and art directors.

When you have your answers, write them down and set them aside. Once you've done this exercise you can more or less forget about it for now. You will want to refer to your answers later as a sounding board for ideas and executions. Before that, it's time to encourage some creativity. Creativity isn't going to be found in your strategic thinking; it's going to come from the other half of your brain.

1//

2//

1// Esteban Muñoz,
estebanmunoz.com
Esteban's black and white line drawings provide an imaginative moving landscape to offset the colorful work in his portfolio.

2// Camelia Dobrin,
camellie.com
Here, the detail views allow scrolling while the background illustration stays motionless—a simple effect that, combined with Camelia's intricate drawing style, helps this portfolio stand out from the crowd.

Find inspiring reference material

1//

2//

3//

To create great things you need to get inspired. Good ideas and execution don't happen in a vacuum. The most prolific creative people surround themselves with the things that inspire them, both manmade and from nature.

Look for inspiration beyond the boundaries of other people's creative output. Keep your eyes open for patterns and structures in the real world that you can weave into your concepts, metaphors, and portfolio architecture. Keep a camera and a sketchpad with you when you're out and about to capture ideas and images.

It's a good idea to create an ongoing reference library as a repository of information. It can be digital, analog, or both. Grab anything and everything you like, from images off the web to pages from magazines, along with your own sketches and photos, and keep all of it on file. When a new project comes up, such as the creation of an innovative and effective digital portfolio, you'll have an existing library to dip into when gathering inspiration.

You'll want to categorize your reference material into groupings that make sense for the disciplines on which you focus. Group examples of great ideas together. Group examples of amazing typography together. Group illustrations together. This will make it easier when you need to find inspiration in a hurry.

When gathering visual inspiration, moodboards are useful tools for aggregating and focusing your effort. Create collages from groupings of designs, illustrations, photos, and textures to indicate different visual directions you want to explore and compare.

Here are a handful of useful sources of inspiration:

Flickr, flickr.com
The ultimate social network for photographers. Searching the entire Flickr universe and sorting by most to least interesting is a great way to get visually inspired.

Ffffound!, ffffound.com
An image bookmarking service, Ffffound! lets you browse image by image and find visual and conceptual inspiration. Registration is invitation only, but anyone can browse the site.

The FWA: Favourite Website Awards, thefwa.com
An awards showcase that attracts a huge majority of the best advertising microsites, portfolio sites, unique content sites, and more. Browse the site of the day, month, and year winners and prepare to be blown away.

The Behance Network, behance.net
One of the creative social networks reviewed in this book (see page 36), Behance contains a great number of portfolio sites and creative profiles. Browse the community for design and illustration inspiration.

Vimeo, vimeo.com
Originally created by creative film and video people, Vimeo is a video-based community offering inspiring moving images.

Twitter Search, search.twitter.com
Searching the Twitter universe can be useful for reference-gathering on a specific topic. Try typing in "cool portfolio," for example, and see what comes up. Following other creative professionals is also a good way to pick up inspirational links.

Tech tip
The web is an amazing source of inspiration. Equipped with a screengrabbing tool such as Snagit (available from techsmith.com), you can hunt and gather to your heart's content.

4//

1// Ffffound!, ffffound.com

2// Flickr, flickr.com

3// The FWA: Favourite Website Awards, thefwa.com

4// An example moodboard.

Think broad

At the beginning of the ideas generation stage, think as broadly as possible. It's important to realize that you're trying to produce ideas to solve a problem. Do you have a clear grasp of what problem you are trying to solve? Put it in actual words as an extension of your strategy. This stated problem is the backbone of your brief—you must find solutions to this problem.

1//

2//

Your written problem to solve could come out like one of these:

"Creative directors at design agencies don't know that I have illustration and photography in my repertoire and can think conceptually."

"My dream collaborative music video project is out there and I'm not connected to it yet."

"My brilliant ceramic and textile creations don't have anywhere to live online that accurately reflects their conceptual nature and beauty."

1// *Stream of consciousness writing and word association are good techniques for ideas generation.*

2// *Keeping a sketchpad helps with ideas gathering and refinement.*

When it comes time to brainstorm, consider these tips:

Think back to your strategy and inspiration and then forget all of it. If you're going for something conceptually, it's good at this stage to put yourself in a free-flowing frame of mind.

Stream of consciousness writing is a good way to get things started. Scrawled words quickly turn into sketchy ideas. Don't spend too much time on any one idea. You are thinking broadly at this point and trying to get as many seeds of ideas as possible.

Be positive. The creative process begins with a stage of considering that anything is possible. The minute you hear a voice saying, "That's a bad idea because..." tell it to go away. It's not welcome right now. Some of the best ideas are offshoots of an original seed of an idea that would have sounded absolutely ludicrous at first.

It's very telling that the most creative teams in advertising agencies are almost always the ones who appear to be having the most fun. Laughter is a clear sign that your mind is in the right headspace for becoming ideas-prone.

Gather as many seeds of ideas as you can. Later on you will pick the strongest ones and begin refinement and execution considerations. Keep reminding yourself that you're not looking for the one perfect solution—you're looking for many good solutions. Looking for the one perfect solution is a flawed and impossible quest.

Quick tip

Feeling stuck for ideas? Try these techniques to help unblock your mind:

Reverse the problem. What would you create if you were trying to NOT get work? Try it for a while to see what happens. It may lead to interesting ideas in unexpected ways.

Ask yourself how a five-year-old would solve this problem. Thinking like a child may help to jog ideas loose.

Try switching to a different project and come back to your portfolio concept generation when you've worked on something else for a while.

Lastly, take time to sleep on it. Your brain will be swimming with the challenge of the brief and will continue to process ideas as you rest.

Think tight

1// 2//

Once you have allowed yourself the creative freedom of thinking broadly, where anything goes and no idea is a bad idea, you should end up with a bunch of slightly scattered and ambiguously defined seeds of ideas. If you have been scrawling in a sketchpad, you might find it helpful to transfer the ramblings to pieces of paper you can stick to a wall or scatter on a table. This way you can step back from your own thoughts and prejudices of these ideas and view them objectively.

As you transcribe them to paper, give each idea a short name so they start to form an identity in your mind. When you have your ideas in front of you, start looking for patterns and consolidate them into groups. Possible groupings could be "visual metaphor," "minimal," or "illustrative." Organizing your ideas and comparing them to each other encourages refinement and editing. Ideas that seem to stagnate can be brushed aside and redundant ideas can join forces. Take notes throughout this process as execution ideas come to you.

Work your way toward rating your consolidated ideas from strongest to weakest. Consider trying to isolate your top five ideas to work up in more detail. Which ideas resonate best with you? Which ones do you keep coming back to?

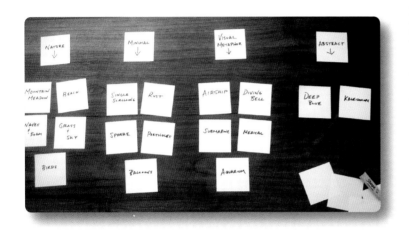

When you have a shortlist, take each idea in turn and jot down more notes and sketches on each to develop them further. Ask yourself questions of each. Do they answer the brief? Do they tie in well with your strategy? Are they innovative enough? Use these criteria to rate and refine them further.

This shortlist of ideas will give you confidence as you proceed with the next steps. You now have not just one but several good ideas. If the one you choose to go ahead with doesn't work out, you have others to fall back on.

If this part of the process has left you frustrated with all of the ideas, step back to thinking broadly and let your mind roam freely again.

1// Write short names for your ideas on pieces of paper with a thick pen to help you visualize them all together.

2// Arrange them in groups to help identify common themes and complementary ideas.

Sketch your ideas

Once you have gathered some inspiration, generated some ideas, and then narrowed them down to a few of your favorite options, it's time to grab a pencil and pad and start sketching your ideas to life. This step is important: if you rush into your usual design tools you may get distracted by execution details, rather than remaining focused on the idea and communication behind the execution. Sketches can also be useful for getting feedback from colleagues. If you can convey the points you're trying to make in sketch form, chances are they will translate well to finished designs.

1// Sketching freely is a good way to continue your creative brainstorming. Keep an open mind as you draw.

2// Switch gears to sketch the underlying architecture of your portfolio site and begin to map it to your concept.

1//

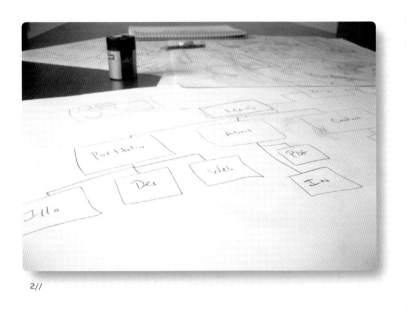

2//

It is important to note that you will also be thinking through (or rethinking) the information architecture of your conceptual portfolio site. This means you will be considering where to put information about yourself, how people will access your work, and how the information about your work will be included. Getting this thought through in the sketching phase will save you time in design.

Move from high-level rough sketches to low-level detailed sketches as a way of rapidly working through conceptual and organizational thinking. This type of conceptual interactive design requires plenty of gear shifting between left and right brain. Remember to go back to your reference material for inspiration.

Quick tip

Sketches of interface design can be used for quick and easy user testing. Grab five friends and set them in front of your sketches one by one. Ask them where they would click if they were looking to check out your work, and what impression the presentation gives them. Are they able to find your contact details?

Pretend they are a potential client who is reviewing your work. Encourage them to think out loud, and make notes on their comments as they go. As they indicate where they would click, you can swap sketches to show them the resulting view they would receive were they looking at your finished site.

Create visual impact

You are competing with a sea of visual communicators, so it's important to create high visual impact for reviewers when they first come to your site. Remember the stage analogy we used earlier? The moment visitors arrive is like the curtain going up on a performance. What will you hit them with first? What visual scenery will they be greeted with?

A good approach is to have your strongest content in front to make that all-important first impression. How you choose to display that work, potentially with snippets of other pieces at the same time, and how you depict the packaging concept you've come up with, are all variables that affect the ultimate visual impact of your site.

1//

2//

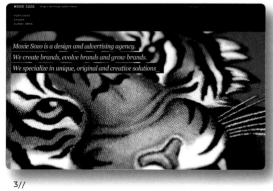

3//

4//

5//

6//

In many cases, your reviewers will be creative professionals themselves and will most likely have fairly large monitor displays. Make the most of this by considering large imagery on the main page and throughout your portfolio, unless there is a specific conceptual reason for displaying your work at a smaller scale.

Revisit your visual inspiration gathering effort and compose moodboards for a visual style that suits what you have in mind. A refined conceptual sketch and an evocative moodboard are excellent foundation tools for moving into Photoshop mockup mode.

As you begin the actual design stage of your creative solution, call on all your skills as a visual communicator to execute your concept. Web pages can be mocked up in any number of programs, but Adobe Photoshop is the industry standard and contains many features specially suited to the tasks at hand.

1// Kashmir Creative, Alex Antuna, kashmircreative.com
Minimalism, beauty, and tension create visual impact on this site.

2// X Producciones Graficas, Javier Castillo, xgraphica.com
Javier lets his content float freely on a rich background texture.

3// Moxie Sozo, moxiesozo.com
Never underestimate the simple power of combining one engaging image with one direct message.

4// Adhemas Batista, adhemas.com
Adhemas knows how to get our attention!

5// Robert Lindström, Designchapel, designchapel.com
Designchapel's front door sets high expectations for imagery, typography, and art direction.

6// Flourish Web Design, floridaflourish.com
Here, a tightly executed visual metaphor is well integrated with both site structure and navigation.

Build a prototype

A prototype enables early visualization of the end result in order to give you the momentum and perspective you need to hone and refine your work-in-progress portfolio site.

Among the many forms it can take are a set of Photoshop mockups linked together via simple HTML image maps such that you and others can click their way through the "site." A prototype can also be an actual XHTML and CSS build that simply isn't wired up to any database or content-management backend. Flash animation prototyping is great to introduce at this stage if you're undertaking that work yourself or collaborating with someone else.

These approaches to designing and building a prototype are powerful because they provide insight without too much throwaway effort. It allows you to take steady steps toward the end goal without too much commitment in a particular direction should you choose to change paths.

A prototype creates another opportunity to invite others for feedback and facilitate some basic user testing. Are people able to find the essential parts of your portfolio?

1// Using software such as Adobe Dreamweaver, create image maps over your mockups to link them together as a click-through prototype.

2// The basic HTML beneath this type of prototype reveals how simple the implementation is when compared to fully developed pages.

1//

2//

Tech tip

If you choose to create designed mockups and link them together via simple HTML image maps, you can also use this prototype as a handy tool for briefing a developer. As they click through the pages, they will be able to better visualize the job to be done.

As you move from this stage into actual final build and execution, you will want to refer to the technical tips section earlier in this book to gain insight into the web development and hosting aspects of creating a portfolio site (see pp. 32-33).

Give someone a task to perform such as, "Find illustration experience and then contact details," and watch them attempt to perform it. If you have designed an intuitive site they should be able to accomplish basic tasks such as this, but watching them tackle the task may lead to useful insight.

As you create designed mockups from your concept work, you might revisit the essential elements discussed earlier in this book to evaluate whether you are first hitting the basic needs of your target audience and then innovating to stand out on top of that.

If you are not happy with how things are shaping up in the design prototyping stage, don't worry. You can always take a few steps back and revisit your ideas shortlist for other directions that may now have renewed appeal. Not happy with your shortlist? Take a step further back from that and think broadly again to generate a new set of ideas. Ideas generation through to prototyping and back again is a productive, iterative process that can be repeated as many times as required to get it right.

Gallery

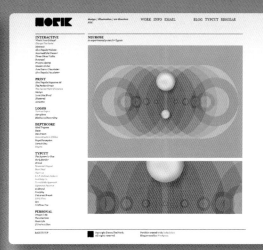

The Norik, thenorik.com
Design, illustration, and art direction
New York City, US
Combination of list navigation and
gallery format (Indexhibit) with blog
(WordPress).

JESSICA HISCHE

TYPE   DESIGN   ILLUSTRATION   BLOG   STORE   ABOUT

TYPE

Daily Drop Cap
Ribbon Type Patterns
Bartholomew Fortuno
Buttermilk Font
Golf Digest
12 Stories of Giving
Sonoma Alphabet
Trashionistas
InStyle Ultimate Beauty Blackbook
You've Got the Spirit...
Personal Posters
Tiffany & Co.
Anneli Hendrix Baby Announcemen
Ruhland & Ruhland
Various Ribbon Type
Brooklyn Type
Romance Novel Type
Chalk Type alphabet
Target
GQ Magazine
Bath and Body Works
Beautiful / Decay

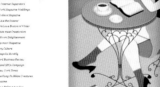

Jessica Hische, jessicahische.com
Typography, design, and illustration
Brooklyn, New York City, US
List navigation format with blog.

Gallery

Rolando Mèndez Acosta,

rolando.com.br

Film and photography director

Brazil

Conceptual format (visual metaphor).

Jeff Vermeersch, vermeersch.ca

Group Head of Interactive, Taxi

Toronto, Canada

Conceptual format

(multidirectional scrolling).

Gallery

Adam Rix, adamrix.com
Design, art direction, and branding
Manchester, UK
Conceptual format (slideshow).
Site built by Jono Brain,
digitalblahblah.com

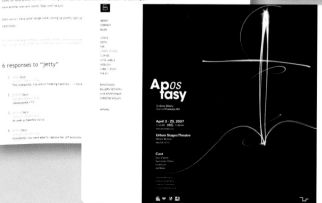

Ray Sison, skilledconcept.com
Art direction, graphic design,
and photography
New York City, US
List navigation format with blog
(WordPress).

CONTENT

CONTENT

CONTENT

Now that you've built a portfolio, how do you decide what to put in it? Choosing exactly what to include is a never-ending challenge. Ideally, you will have the ability to tweak the exact mix easily as this tactic will suit the broadest range of strategies. However, as you approach this next stage we will identify some guidelines that apply to most scenarios.

Your work is not all that your portfolio contains— it is also home to your personal story. The role of additional information will be covered in this section, as well as helpful tips about copyright law and protecting your work. There are certain ethical obligations to be aware of as you move closer toward launching your new site. Chapter Four will cover these as well.

CHAPTER THREE: What to include
Demonstrate your creative process

As you begin to choose what to put in your portfolio, it is helpful to review your strategy and objectives. How important is it for what you're trying to achieve that you provide examples of your creative process? For some creatives it will be mandatory to show how they think and work. For others, it will simply be an opportunity to flesh out their character and perceived capabilities in greater detail.

Art directors, creatives, and others responsible for ideation may want to show sketches and other preliminary output to give an indication of conceptual thinking from brief to solution and from big ideas through to communication execution.

Illustrators may want to show compositional studies and preliminary sketches, depending on the type of work they're going for. An illustrator appealing to other creative professionals may be more inclined to show process than when talking to those with non-creative roles.

Photographers responsible for their own art direction and shooting concepts may want to reveal sketches and schematics indicating how they conceptualize and plan their shoots if they are trying to win collaborative work with other creatives.

1//

If you have developed an innovative technique, you could try documenting this to create a bit of backstory. For example: an artist who has developed their own form of encaustic and mixed media painting may not want to reveal all of their secrets, but showing a few shots of the painting process with simple captions could help give more meaning to the paintings for viewers.

2//

Design tip

It is good to show your work on its own and in context to flesh out the overall picture and demonstrate both the quality of the work and its effectiveness in a practical application.

A simple and seamless way of presenting process is to include early sketches, mockups, prototypes, and other work in progress as detail images mixed inline with the finished work itself. When a reviewer drills down into a project at the detail level, the first few images could be the best finished shots from the project, but as they scroll along deeper the process-related imagery would appear. This gives the effect of peeling back layers of presentation and diving beneath the surface.

The notes that you include with your work are a great opportunity to augment your imagery with information about your process. We'll discuss this more later in the chapter.

One engaging way to document your process is to take video or create a stop-motion effect by shooting stills from a tripod that is positioned in front of where you're working. Strung together in video form, the effect of watching a piece come to life in sped-up time can be exhilarating. There are many great examples of this on the web, especially in the realm of murals and street art.

1// *Maciej Hajnrich, valpnow.com*
Before and after photo illustration.

2// *Jessica Hische, jessicahische.com*
Example of work shown in and out of context.

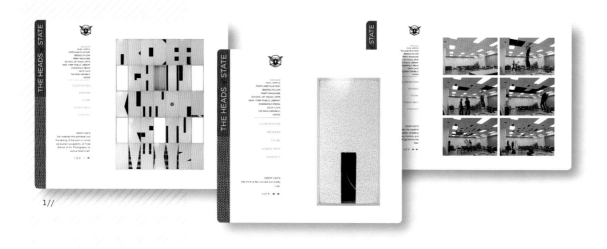

1//

Appealing to other creative professionals by creating step-by-step tutorials is a different approach altogether. You can create content that helps other designers, illustrators, and artists to recreate some of the techniques you have invented or to perform pre-existing tasks and techniques that you have developed a particular mastery of. You will find that good content attracts attention from your peers while demonstrating to potential clients and employers an ability not only to understand complex techniques but to convey that understanding to others.

1// *Heads of State,*

theheadsofstate.com

Typography installation in ceiling.

2// *Jelle Gijsberts,*

jellepelle.nl/archives/282

Illustration tutorial video.

3// *Oleg Kostuk,*

theoleg.com

Process animations.

4// *Toby Caves,*

phigerone.com

Video post-production.

The Making of an Illustration

11 Comments »

In the video on the left you can see the making of one of my illustrations. I recorded my desktop during the creation of a scene where a cowboy enters a saloon. The original rendering process took me around 5 hours, and it's sped up here to about 15 minutes.

2//

Tutorials can take the form of text and images or animation and video. Use screen-capture software such as Camtasia from TechSmith (techsmith.com) when documenting processes on the computer for video output. See notes on working with video later in this chapter.

One word of caution: Make sure you are not simply pointing out the obvious unless your tutorials are clearly aimed at beginners, as this can seem amateurish.

3//

4//

Illustrate your range

Are you looking for a specialist role or a generalist role? What is your potential employer or client looking for? What does your strategy tell you?

You may have work across several disciplines. You may have work from your art and design classes. You may have personal projects. The key to illustrating your range is providing a clear structure, labeling, and navigation so people can find what they're looking for. Refer back to the sections on information architecture (pages 48–49) and navigation design (pages 50–51).

Some creative disciplines complement each other more than others. With these combinations it is less of a stretch for reviewers to grasp that you have abilities in both, and more importantly, how they can make the most of your broad range should they choose to hire you. For example, illustration and graphic design go hand in hand in many ways. Graphic design makes great use of illustration, and good illustration relies on the same principles of composition and color harmony that graphic design does.

1//

In other cases, the connections between disciplines may not be so straightforward and should be considered thoughtfully. If two disciplines are not naturally harmonious there may be a slight conflict of interest. Reviewers need to feel confident that you are an expert in the discipline they may want to hire you for. If you place equal weight on two discipline areas in your repertoire and one of those areas does not gracefully gel with the area they are investigating, they may question your commitment to the original discipline.

An example of two disciplines not typically associated with one another might be painting and product design. Is this a problem worth losing sleep over? Probably not. But if you have an odd collection of disciplines, consider leading with one of them and having the others take a back seat. This simple act of hierarchy clarification can shift perception entirely, moving from potential dissonance to, "This professional has depth of abilities."

In most cases, you will want to choose the work that best illustrates your entire range of abilities. If there is a common visual style across your work regardless of the discipline area, you're especially in luck. An effective presentation style can be to run all of the work together as long as it flows as an inspiring "feed" of your creative spark. A navigation device that allows viewers to filter your work by discipline can be a good complement to this approach. In the case of a long scrolling page format, a list of categories in the footer of each page for filtering the work is a concise way of indicating your broad range.

2//

3//

1// Zeebee Visual Communications, zeebee.co.uk
Example of conceptual navigation system illustrating a range of disciplines.

2// Johnnydoes, johnnydoes.nl
Example of clear discipline labeling to illustrate range.

3// Resn, resn.co.nz
Straightforward listing of capabilities to illustrate range.

Your site's navigation is one of the most immediate opportunities to illustrate your range. Providing clearly labeled sections to your gallery such that viewers can browse your work by discipline is an effective tactic when backed by a sufficient amount of quality work. Avoid creating discipline buckets that you can't back up, as the effect can be one of mismanaged expectations. Put another way: don't over-promise and under-deliver.

Creating multiple portfolios is a good tactic for gathering interest from different networks and industry niches. One way to do this is to have a main portfolio at an address related to your name, then multiple presences in creative social networks such as Behance and Flickr. This way you focus your particular skills and styles at the audiences most receptive to each direction. Anyone who is exploring your talents in depth will get a sense of your range at their own pace as they follow links from one portfolio to another. Multiple versions of your portfolio at different addresses can also be useful for tweaking the contents to prepare for different interviews and pitches.

1// Darek Nyckowiak, thetoke.com
Infographic display of capabilities
by discipline.

2// Paul Lee Design,
paulleedesign.com
Example of a seamless style across
more than one discipline.

3// Darren Whittington,
digitalvsprint.com
Example of slideshow videos to display
a range of work in a small area.

1//

It is important to realize that you shouldn't put all of your work in your portfolio just because you can. An overwhelmed and confused reviewer is not an impressed reviewer. Focus is good, and so is consistency. In the eyes of many potential clients and employers, you are only as good as your weakest piece. If you are uncomfortable with a particular work sample for whatever reason, take it out. Refer to the topic "How much is too much?" later in this chapter.

Q: What general advice would you give regarding choosing what to show?

"Show what you are proud of. It kills me when I ask someone about something in their book and they say they don't really like that piece or that it's not their strongest. Take it out. Only show your best. If that means only a few pieces, you should probably work on it some more."
—Blake Kidder, Associate Creative Director, TBWA\ Chiat\Day, Los Angeles

2//

3//

A tightly focused portfolio

Some jobs require generalists. Some jobs require specialists. Sometimes it's good to show a range of skills. Sometimes it's good to show that you have dived deep within a particular area of expertise.

It's important to do your homework. Know your objective and your target audience, as discussed in Section One, and have the ability to change the content of your portfolio quickly and easily to adjust it for specific pitches and interviews.

An example of a scenario where you may want to show some specialization in your portfolio might be if you are responding to a very specific job advertisement and other areas of your body of work don't complement the specialization very well. If you have typography-oriented graphic design in your portfolio but also dabble in character illustration, when applying for a job that requires traditional graphic design ability you might focus your core portfolio on the typographic work.

At some point in your career, it will probably no longer be appropriate to include student work in your portfolio. Including student work much longer than three years into your career may raise a red flag with reviewers. After that time, there should be sufficient real work to draw on to fill

1//

2//

3//

your portfolio. If this isn't the case, consider inventing your own assignments, as "Personal Project" is a less alarming label than "Student Work." We'll discuss techniques for developing new work for your portfolio later in this chapter.

However much work you decide to put into your portfolio, give a thought to the way the arrangement of your work flows. As if you were composing a showreel, take care that each piece sits naturally with the pieces before and after it. As discussed, lead with something strong. It's also good to finish with a bang, so a standard trick is to put your second-best piece last. Be wary that if you put too much in your portfolio the reviewer may not get that far.

1// *Toothjuice, Josh Clancy,*
toothjuice.net
Example of a tightly focused
one-page illustration portfolio.

2// *Louise Fili, louisefili.com*
A tightly focused packaging and
graphic design portfolio.

3// *Maciej Hajnrich,*
flickr.com/photos/valp00
Use of Flickr to create tightly
focused image sets.

How much is too much?

Too many pieces in your portfolio may indicate to a reviewer that you have difficulty seeing the big picture, may be lacking fundamental editing skills, and may be overly self-centered. A general guide is to keep the number of projects featured in the main part of your portfolio to between ten and twenty. There's plenty of opportunity to show more than one image or other piece of media per project, so this quantity should be easily accommodated and still provide great depth of content.

It is also helpful for the reviewer to know at all times how far into your collection they are and how much further it is to the end. This comes down to basic web usability.

It can be useful to be able to quickly shuffle your work around depending on what type of interview you are going into.

2//

1//

Here are some tips to help you edit:

If you are not thrilled with a piece for any reason, leave it out. Chances are if you're not that into it, reviewers won't be either.

Be wary of putting in work that you don't like doing but that you think will help you get a job. You will most likely get more of that kind of work.

Avoid repetition. If you have several pieces that demonstrate similar skills, consider paring them down and balance those pieces with other examples from your repertoire.

Remember that you can always organize your portfolio into sections by discipline if you have a large body of work across multiple areas. This will provide focus and allow the reviewer to take control of the experience and see what they want to see.

Similarly, you can have your strongest work in the main set of your portfolio and everything that didn't make the cut in a separate set as an appendix. That way if a reviewer asks to see more work of a particular type you have something on hand to show them.

Q: How much work should people include in their portfolio?

"For me, it's the first five to eight examples that do ninety percent of the work, so I'd say fifteen to twenty examples is the maximum amount."
—Iain McDonald, Founder, Amnesia Razorfish, Australia

1// *Form Troopers,*
formtroopers.com
Example of including multiple pieces in one view to condense the overall presentation.

2// *Proud Creative,*
proudcreative.com
Example of good editing and organizing to cover a wide area with relatively few projects.

Developing new work for your portfolio

Is your portfolio feeling light? Want to stretch your abilities and get more of the kind of work you like to do? Do something about it by creating work specifically for your portfolio. Track down portfolios that you admire and create assignments to fill yours with work that emulates what you like and the kind of work you want to get paid to do. Refer to the inspiration-gathering topic in Chapter Two to find inspiring portfolios.

Employers looking to hire into more junior positions understand that it's tough to fill a portfolio with paid work when you are starting out or making a career change, and they will admire your drive if you create your own assignments to improve your skills.

You might try approaching a made-up assignment just like you would a paid gig. Make sure there is a clear brief and a deadline. An indefinite timeframe isn't ideal if you are trying to fill your portfolio and get work quickly.

1//

2//

When creating an assignment for yourself, it can be helpful to consider the following:

Invent an achievable brief
Choose something that might exist in the real world that is similar to the type of work you want to get paid for. Make it realistic; something you can achieve. Make it specific and have it play to your strengths.

Prepare
Find the right inspiration by browsing other portfolios for the type of work you would like to do. Break down their techniques and experiment with emulating them. Read online tutorials and practice the techniques discussed. You'll find useful resources at *clazie.com/digitalportfolios.*

Give yourself a deadline
A backburner project will always stay on the backburner if the timer never goes off. Micromanage yourself and set small milestones to break the job into achievable chunks.

1// *GrandArmy for Wieden+Kennedy, grand-army.com Inspirational proactivity: The Nike Wild Pitch. "A proposal asking Nike to resurrect their cult classic McFly 2015 sneakers featured in Back To The Future 2. They did."*

2// *Personal projects of Adhemas Batista, adhemas.com*

Get feedback

When you have something that a colleague can review, be it a sketch or the finished piece, seek feedback and be open-minded. Encourage them to be honest. Grow a thick skin. Taking feedback well is one of the most important qualities of a good creative professional.

Have several irons in the fire

If you get a mental block it can be helpful to have a few other projects going, especially ones that exercise different parts of your brain. This allows you to mentally move around and loosen things up. Gathering reference material for your library or contributing to a blog can make suitable unblockers.

Collaborating with other creative professionals in similar situations can be a great way to pool resources and energy. You will find a number of ways to connect with like-minded individuals on creative social networks such as Behance.

Taking on a crowdsourcing challenge can be another way for graphic and web designers to fill their portfolios rapidly if they are okay with doing work on spec (working with the understanding that you might not get paid). As we said previously (see pages 66–67), this is a fairly controversial topic. Read up on the debate before deciding whether to participate in crowdsourcing.

1//

2//

3//

If you decide to try it out, visit one of the popular design-oriented platforms such as crowdSPRING (crowdspring.com) and search the competitions. Find one you are confident about and try your hand. If you don't win, hopefully you will wind up with a piece that may be suitable for your portfolio.

In addition, there are many creative competitions going at any one time. Entering these is another powerful incentive for creating your own work without a client.

1// HunterGatherer,
Todd St. John, huntergatherer.net
Promotional T-shirts.

2// Nelson Balaban,
xtrabold.net
Experimental typographic illustration.

3// Kris Robinson,
oinkfu.com
A collaborative illustration
contest submission.

Preparing images for digital viewing

If your work is not in digital form, you will need to digitize it so it can be included in your portfolio site. Your choices for digitizing physical creative pieces are either to photograph them or to scan them.

If you work with a service bureau that provides professional scanning services, scanning may be the winner for overall simplicity and ease for work that is completely flat. Still photography with correct lighting equipment and a good camera will generally yield higher-quality results, however.

When you have successfully created digital images of your pieces, you will ideally have 300dpi or higher resolution source files in an uncompressed format with which to work. TIFF is a suitable format to scan or save to. If JPEG format is your only option for source files, make sure the compression quality is set to maximum or very high at the least.

Once you have a collection of source files of your work, you can output web-ready JPEG or PNG files to the dimensions required by your portfolio design. Web browsers commonly support three image formats: JPEG, PNG, and GIF. As the latter is most suitable for digital native graphics of a certain appearance it is rare that digitized imagery will be better optimized in this format.

1//

2//

Compare the formats yourself with your own images and choose the option you think gives the best results. If using JPEG compression, remember that this is a portfolio site and you want your work to look good. With today's high-speed internet connections, in most scenarios setting your images to very high JPEG quality is fine as far as file size optimization is concerned.

Standard screen resolution (the number of dots per inch on a computer's screen) is 72dpi. When saving out web-ready images from your source files, use this resolution and remember to not save over your source files. You will want to keep them at their full resolution for later use.

1// Moxie Sozo,

moxiesozo.com

Taking quality photographs of printed pieces from multiple angles creates an opportunity to construct new compositions and get more mileage and depth out of your work.

2// Matt Titone,

matttitone.com

Here, multiple pieces from one project are arranged to form the appearance of a naturally occurring collage.

Shooting for your portfolio

1//

If you are shooting flat artwork or printed designs, you must shoot for quality and with the correct equipment and environment. For your portfolio, the right content shot in the wrong way will fail to get the attention it deserves.

Shooting two-dimensional objects is relatively easy. Shooting them well is a bit of a challenge and requires some specific skills too involved to cover completely here. Shooting three-dimensional objects is an even greater challenge, as there's a much heavier burden on optimal lighting and other factors. Get it right and you have an excellent opportunity to add beauty, warmth, and depth to your portfolio.

The most reliable and straightforward approach may be to hire a professional photographer who has experience of shooting artwork and design. If you would rather do it yourself, here's a list of the equipment you will need:

1. A digital SLR camera with a good zoom lens (to fill the frame with the artwork) and a polarizing filter (to help reduce glare)
2. Two powerful floodlights
3. Two lightstands
4. Diffusion covers for the lights
5. A camera tripod
6. An exposure meter
7. A vertical level

Some general guidelines to bear in mind when shooting:

Color balance is very important and can be difficult to correct after shooting, so pay attention to the camera's color settings.

Shoot in manual mode and bracket the exposure by going half, one, one and a half, and then two stops over and under the recommended reading.

Fill the camera frame with the subject matter as opposed to leaving a large area around it. This helps keep the digital image dimensions parallel with the original.

2//

Hang the work on a wall and use a level to position the camera in front of the piece such that the lens is pointing at the piece in a line directly parallel to the floor.

Use a suitable backdrop such as neutral-colored paper so as not to detract from the work.

Angle your lights at 45 degrees to the subject matter to avoid glare.

1// Jan Pautsch.Lilienthal,

thismortalmagic.com

A subtle twist on the popular

technique of holding a printed piece

for the camera with face obscured.

Tweak your images in Photoshop (while viewed on a well-calibrated monitor) for any final color balance and contrast adjustments required.

2// 25ah, 25ah.se

The arrangement of these printed

pieces becomes like a casual group of

musicians in a candid group portrait.

A common technique for three-dimensional work (or any printed work where it is useful to show the scale and physicality of the piece) is to shoot the object while holding it in front of you. With your face out of the frame to avoid distraction, the effect can be quite compelling and humanizing when shot in good quality.

Scanning

Digitizing your flat creative pieces with a scanner can be done professionally by a service bureau or at home with a store-bought scanner. Professional scanners provide higher quality than most affordable home scanners. Professional services usually accommodate oversized pieces as well.

If quality and size are a major concern, consider locating a professional scanning service provider near you. However, if you have a scanner at home and prefer this method, here are some tips:

- Before you scan, clean the surface with glass cleaner and a clean, soft cloth. Allow to dry.
- Make sure that the edges of your work are parallel to the edges of your scanner.
- When scanning pieces that are thick and therefore lift the scanner lid up, allowing light to creep in, drape a dark cloth over the piece instead of closing the lid.
- Even though you are preparing images for display at 72dpi, scan at a higher resolution so you have more to work with. Consider a minimum of 300dpi.

If you need to scan anything larger than the scanner bed area, scan in sections and use Photoshop to "stitch" together the pieces. Bring each segment scan into the same PSD as different layers and make sure they are rotationally aligned. Set the top layer blending mode to Difference and position it correctly over the layer beneath it until the overlapping area turns completely black.

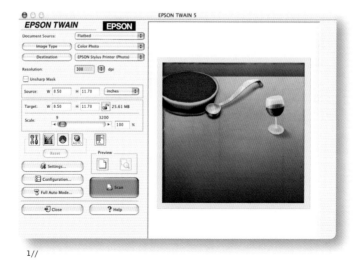

1//

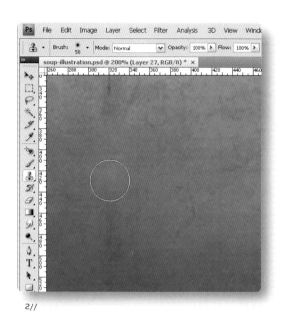
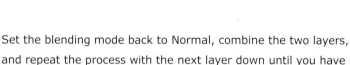

2//

Quick tip

There is no substitute
for getting it right with
a good scan in the first
place, so be wary of
setting yourself up for an
impossible retouching
task and consider using
a professional service if
you have a poor-quality
scanner at home.

Set the blending mode back to Normal, combine the two layers, and repeat the process with the next layer down until you have created one seamless layer.

Photoshop can be used for a myriad other post-scanning purposes, including using the clone tool to repair unwanted folds or creases in paper and other blemishes. Color balance is a prime area of concern when working with an inferior-quality scanner. Some color correction is possible with Photoshop; it is best to have the actual piece next to you when you attempt to address any color issues.

1// *Typical scanner settings.*

2// *Using Adobe Photoshop's clone tool to remove a crease.*

Working with video

There are a few reasons to consider putting video into your portfolio site:

If you are a motion graphics designer, an animator, or in any way involved with creative output that consists of moving imagery, a video showreel is a mandatory element in your portfolio and there is a strong case for leading off with it.

If you have created something that people interact with in real life in a way that is interesting and helps tell your story, you may want to shoot video of that real-world involvement. If you have case studies that can be summarized in an easy-to-digest video format with simple shots interspersed with text and live-action video to tell the story of a project from brief to results, this can be a great storytelling tool. Tutorials indicating process and studio techniques can also be captured in video form.

Some things to consider in all cases:

Keep it short. As with the rest of your portfolio, it helps to be direct and edit down to your best work and most valid points. The only items that might run longer are ones in a feature, documentary, or seminar format. Consider keeping a showreel down to between one and three minutes and never more than five.

If you are going to do something unusual or innovative with the video format, do it well. Out-there ideas poorly executed will do you more harm than good. Avoid cheesy out-of-the-box

1//

2//

transitions and effects, especially if you are putting a showreel together. The hiring creative professionals viewing your reel or other video will be able to discern the techniques that are flashy-looking but require no skill. It's not a good look.

Adobe After Effects is a popular software package for bringing static imagery to life for display in video form. In the hands of skilled motion graphics professionals it can be used to create serious magic. If you're up for a new challenge, visit the Adobe site, download the trial, and follow a beginner's tutorial. Remember that it is easy to be blinded by the wonders of creative technology when it's new to you. Make sure you stay realistic about how rough or polished the end result may look before you choose to include it in your portfolio.

If you are creating video for your site, pay attention to some common techniques and fundamentals of motion storytelling and video editing. Some basic building blocks you'll want to consider:

1. An introduction during which the title of the video is presented.
2. Put your strongest work first to make a good impression and get viewers interested.
3. A suitable soundtrack and any appropriate sound effects.
4. Seamless transitions between projects.
5. Movement and timing that has a suitable energy level for the effect you are trying to achieve.
6. A conclusion during which your identity or the title of the video is again presented.

There are a large number of inspirational showreels on the web. Find a few at *clazie.com/digitalportfolios.*

3//

1// *HunterGatherer,*

huntergatherer.net

HunterGatherer's beautifully simple

creations come to life in their

animated form. When highlights

are edited together into a showreel,

their creators' skills are demonstrated

quickly and clearly.

2// *Form Troopers,*

formtroopers.com

As motion graphics is a core discipline

for Form Troopers, they dedicate an

entire section of their portfolio to it

while still leading off with a showreel

of highlights.

3// *North Kingdom Showreel 2009,*

via Designchapel, designchapel.com

This showreel weaves a storyline

throughout the presentation of

the work—a technique that justifies

a slightly longer format.

Stating your objective

There are several opportunities within a digital portfolio to tell your story and give background information that gives visitors a bigger picture of where you are coming from and where you are looking to go. It is important for potential clients to understand something about you so they can feel confident about working with you.

Cultural fit is a high priority for employers when reviewing candidates for a role. It doesn't matter how talented you are if you're a nightmare to be around. Let your personality come forward when you tell your story, but keep it professional—personal and friendly, but not over the top.

Possibly the most important information to convey quickly and easily is what you do and what you are looking to do. If they are one and the same, that's great. If they are in sync with the work you are displaying, even better. If not on both counts, you will need to be tactful in your word choice and make sure you don't introduce contradictions that will leave readers feeling confused.

Remember when talking about what you do and what you are looking for that if you are looking for employment you shouldn't position yourself as a business. Save that for if you are looking for clients and want to appear to have the weight of more than just one person. Potential employers can be put off if they feel they are hiring someone who may have a competing business to run.

As discussed in Chapter One, it's important to be clear and direct when stating your objective. The purpose of your objective is for potential clients or employers to pick up the following:

1. That you are motivated and professional.
2. What your strengths and capabilities are.
3. What you are interested in doing more of.
4. Your location.

1//   2//

If your objective is short enough—and concise is good—it can sit in the header of your site accompanying your identity. Combined in this way it becomes an extension, or in a way a definition, of your identity. Other appropriate analogies would be the job title on your business card or the tagline if you were a product for sale.

An example of a simple identity extension:

Ian Clazie
Digital Design Director, Sydney

An example of a more elaborate objective statement:

Ian Clazie
Freelance digital interactive design and art direction based in Sydney, Australia

Another approach is to list the services you provide like this:

Visual Design
Interaction Design
Art Direction
Illustration
Copywriting

The benefit of this approach is that viewers can easily take the information in when quickly scanning the page.

3//

1// Toy, toyny.com
Toy's introductory statement establishes a link between their name and their philosophy.

2// Oscar Barber, oscarbarber.com
As prominently as he can, Oscar says who he is, what he does, and where he does it.

3// Fat-Man Collective, fat-man-collective.com
Possibly one of the clearest examples of how to weave information about a company into a web interface.

Project descriptions

1//

2//

What you write to describe each project in your portfolio is a key part of telling your story. Reviewers will want to know exactly what role you played in creating the visuals before them. They will want to know the nature of the brief and the insight you brought to your solutions. They will also want to get an idea of how you communicate, what your personality is like, and how professional you are overall.

Some general guidelines:

Consider a tone of voice that is friendly but professional; be warm but not overly familiar. Let your personality come through, but don't go overboard.

Be concise. You want to convey the important information quickly. No one wants to sit and read a novel online.

Being professional means no typos or grammatical errors. Also avoid using texting shorthand unless it is essential to your image for some reason.

If you are showing work that you created as part of a team or partnership, it is best to focus on the aspects you were responsible for. Being completely transparent about what you did and didn't create is essential.

Remember that project descriptions are a good opportunity to provide details and background on your process and methods.

Structure your descriptions consistently so they are easy to scan.

Here's a breakdown of elements to consider:

3//

Project title

The highest-priority element to include, the project title can convey a lot of information when well constructed.

Client name

Whether the work was done directly for a client or done through an agency, there is always a client. If the project was personal, indicate that here, as the client was essentially yourself.

Your role

Indicate any and all roles you performed on this project specifically. Be clear and honest.

The brief

What was the problem that needed solving (expressed in the most concise terms possible)?

Key insight

What was the most important observation revealed in your preparation that helped lead to a solution?

Your solution

Describe the approach you took to answering the brief.

Results

How did the end result perform? Was the client happy? Were commercial objectives met?

Relevant links

Links to any relevant web-based information or sites with explanatory labels.

1// Fat-Man Collective,

fat-man-collective.com

An example of an easily interpreted project description, complete with external links to the other companies involved.

2// Ribbons of Red,

ribbonsofred.com

Listing project deliverables in a consistent location above each description educates visitors at a glance.

3// Johnnydoes,

johnnydoes.nl

Johnnydoes tags each project with the categories it falls in. This not only helps transmit information about services provided, but also helps with site navigation.

Case studies

1//

2//

Some creative professionals make major contributions in ways that aren't as obvious as others. Art directors, creatives, architects, interior designers, and copywriters, to name just a few, are all involved in the ideas and inner workings of creative projects. In many cases they are responsible for tackling complex briefs and breaking the big problem into smaller problems, performing research, and providing insight. Their efforts are not necessarily as visible as the designer or illustrator's, as they may not have as much hands-on involvement with the finished piece. These professionals can benefit from a more elaborate format for using project descriptions to tell their story: the case study.

A case study is an opportunity to drill deeper into a project for the benefit of a reviewer who is thoroughly checking your thinking and conceptual ability. Quite often this is a technique that is more suitable to people in senior positions, as they are often the generals behind the front lines.

A typical case study will include a structure similar to simple project descriptions discussed on pages 118–119, but the amount of detail can be much greater; points can be elaborated on with supporting captioned imagery and explanatory videos.

The areas you'll want to explain in detail will be:

The brief

What exactly was the problem to be solved? Go into more background detail in a case study than you would in a simple project description.

Key insight

What key piece of insight did you bring to the table from your research? Explain in brief how you arrived at this insight.

Your solution

How did you solve the problem? Provide methodologies and techniques used to achieve the solution.

Results

How was the effectiveness of the solution measured and how did it stack up? Provide supporting statistics and sources.

Keep your language and tone clear, concise, and professional when writing case studies. Always proofread what you write carefully. Typos reflect poorly on your professionalism and attention to presentation. Errors in your text reflect the fact that you move too fast and don't understand the value of clear and carefully presented communication. These are not details. They are essentials.

1// *Positive Hype,*

positivehype.com

Including a client testimonial at the head of a case study can be an effective marketing technique.

2// *The Keystone Design Union,*

thekdu.com

The emphasis in this case study is clearly on the photography that demonstrates not only the artwork created, but the overall experience around The KDU's participation.

3// *Firstborn,*

firstbornmultimedia.com

Firstborn has a large number of case studies, making consistent treatment of the information critical.

Biography and resumé

Quick tip

A common scenario ahead of a job interview finds a reviewer rushing to your site to find and print your resumé quickly in the moments before your meeting. For this reason, it is important to make it very easy to locate and print your resumé.

In website speak, your "bio" or biography will generally sit on a page called "about." This page can contain a number of elements for fleshing out your profile. A short bio or description of your experience, skills, and current status (are you looking for work and if so what kind?) is the standard core content for your "about" page. If you want to put a face to the name you can include a profile photo. Clear links to your detailed work history in the form of a resumé are also at home here, as well as a list of awards and honors. This is the place to display those trophies you've collected.

Remember to convey a positive and friendly but professional tone. As always, proofread your writing to avoid mistakes. If you decide to include a photo, make it a good one that says something about you. If you are open and outgoing, choose a portrait style that conveys this.

Including your resumé is important if your objective is to find employment. Potential employers will definitely want to check your work experience and education, along with information on referrals. If you are positioning yourself as a business, however, a resumé can be a confusing inclusion. More appropriate in this case may be a list of past and present clients and relevant credentials.

A common way to include your resumé that ensures ease of printing is to link to it as a PDF in a new window. Be sure to give an indication near the link that this is what visitors can expect when they click.

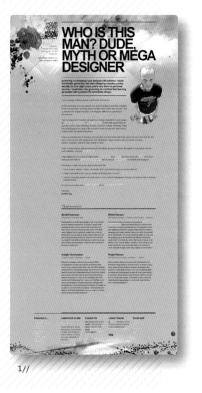

1//

The popular career networking service LinkedIn is another good option for presenting your resumé. Simply sign up for your free account if you don't already have one, fill in your profile details, and link to your profile from your "about" page.

Lastly, remember to provide a prominent link to your contact information, as this is one of the key functions of your site—allowing interested people to get in touch with you. We'll talk about contact information in more detail later in this chapter.

Q: How important is written information about the person (a bio or an "about" page) and why?

"I like to know what people do outside the industry. Often someone's knowledge in sports, film, music, or whatever they are passionate about becomes an asset to the agency and their work."
—Blake Kidder, Associate Creative Director, TBWA\ Chiat\Day, Los Angeles

2//

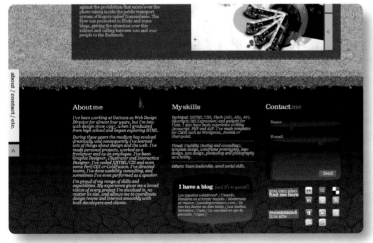

3//

1// Guðmundur Bjarni Sigurðsson, gummisig.com
An "about" page that includes testimonials from colleagues.

2// Adhemas Batista, adhemas.com
Adhemas tells his complete story, but all points return to his belief that he "is selling colors."

3// Juan Diego Velasco, juandiegovelasco.com
An example of concise information about the creator in a site's footer.

Keeping a blog

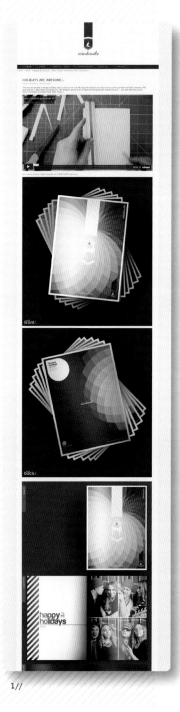

1//

Keeping a blog as an addition to your portfolio is an excellent way not only to tell more of your story, but to generate additional interest, buzz, comments, and links to your site and profile.

Feel like you have nothing to say? Don't worry. Contrary to perception, blogging is not just for those who like the sight of their own words. A blog can also be a useful tool for collecting inspiration and research. Approached this way, over time your blog will become a library of useful and beautiful things that you can refer back to time and again and point people to as needed.

The end result of having a blog relative to finding work is that potential clients and employers can see and hear how you think and what makes you tick. Rather than simply stating in your bio that you are engaged in the design or cultural community, you can demonstrate it beyond a shadow of a doubt.

Author's note: I am writing this book because the publisher's commissioning editor found a post on my blog offering advice on the topic of digital portfolios and came to me with the idea for the book.

Some guidelines to keep in mind when blogging:

Always run a quick check on your topic before posting to see how old the news is and how much buzz there has already been about it. If you are blogging about something that is five years old but you have only just come across it, introducing it with words like "an oldie but goodie" instead of "new amazing site" may be advisable.

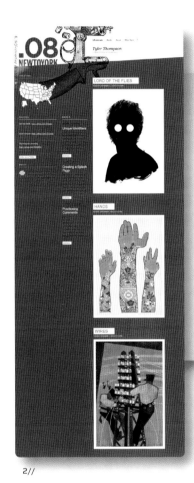

3//

2//

1// MIND Castle Blog,

mindcastleblog.com

MIND Castle's photographs of their

creative process form beautiful stories.

2// New to York, Tyler Thompson,

newtoyork.com

This blog is dominated by a Tumblr-

style feed of inspirational imagery.

3// The Norik Blog,

blog.thenorik.com

The Norik blogs about the inspiration

he finds, in addition to news about his

own work.

If you are blogging about something you have read on someone else's blog, it is ethical to give credit to the original article. As you become more comfortable with blogging as a publishing platform, try adding value to content that you collect by writing introductions, offering insight, perspective, and connections to other information. Some of the most popular blog posts collect multiple references and provide insight tying them together.

Contact information

Providing clear and obvious contact information in your portfolio site is essential if you want to capture the interest that your work generates and turn it into business opportunities.

Providing multiple options for making contact is the best approach. In addition to the more standard forms of contact, such as listing your email address and phone number, it is a good idea to provide a contact form that makes for even easier contact—all people have to do is fill in the blanks and hit send. A form also lets you control what information is provided. If you choose, you can ask visitors who wish to contact you to provide their name, company name, email address, and phone number.

If you are nervous about putting your primary contact details online where anyone can get them, just go with the contact form alone. There is some risk that publishing your email address on your site will result in increased junk mail in your inbox.

1//

2//

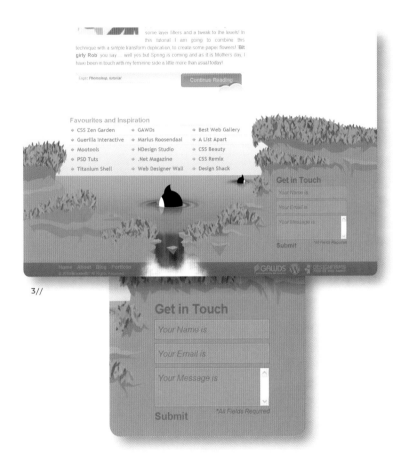

some layer filters and a tweak to the levels! In this tutorial I am going to combine this technique with a simple transform duplication, to create some paper flowers! **Bit girly Rob** you say ... well yes but Spring is coming and as it is Mothers day, I have been in touch with my feminine side a little more than usual today!

Tags: Photoshop, tutorial

Continue Reading

Favourites and Inspiration

- CSS Zen Garden
- Guerilla Interactive
- Mootools
- PSD Tuts
- Titanium Shell

- GAWDs
- Marius Roosendaal
- NDesign Studio
- .Net Magazine
- Web Designer Wall

- Best Web Gallery
- A List Apart
- CSS Beauty
- CSS Remix
- Design Shack

Get in Touch

Your Name is

Your Email is

Your Message is

Submit   *All Fields Required*

Home   About   Blog   Portfolio

3//

Get in Touch

Your Name is

Your Email is

Your Message is

Submit   *All Fields Required*

Most hosting providers offer basic tools for creating contact forms. Sometimes referred to as feedback forms, they will collect the information people provide and send it to your email address without exposing your address to the visitor.

Remember that if your strategy is to generate business directly with clients, it is essential that you are easily contactable via your site. As visitors navigate through your portfolio site, contacting you should be their final action.

1// *Form Troopers,*
formtroopers.com
Form Troopers demonstrate that
a contact page doesn't need to
look boring.

2// *magneticNorth (mN),*
mnatwork.com
On this site, map, contact form, and
contact details are found all in one
view available from any page.

3// *Rob Palmer,*
branded07.com
Rob has a minimal contact form in
the footer of his pages—a friendly
and simple approach.

CHAPTER FOUR: Legalities and ethics
Work done for a previous employer

1//

Generally speaking, and as long as a contractual clause does not strictly forbid it, artists and designers have the right to include work in their portfolio that was created for a previous employer or client.

Like a resumé, your portfolio is proof of your job experience. An employer may ask you to sign a non-compete agreement, which normally lasts for a set amount of time (for example, a year from your last day of employment), in order to prevent the direct reuse of any design concepts or material created and paid for by them or their clients. Most designers will, of course, act professionally and not recycle creative work in this way, but it's a standard inclusion in most contracts.

A non-compete contract may also state that you do not have the right to publicly exhibit any work created for that employer's client, and this includes using that material in your portfolio. In most cases, and as long as you did not leave your previous employment under difficult circumstances, a phone call or email can clear up any issues regarding the right to show your work to prospective new employers. Unpublished work that was not accepted by a client presents more of a problem as the client would not wish to be, in their eyes, misrepresented in any way.

DISCLAIMER: The advice offered in this book is for informational purposes only. Consult a legal professional for actionable advice.

It is always best to review your employment contract closely. If there are any non-compete clauses that concern you or seem overly restrictive, talk them over with your employer and discuss alternatives before you sign. If an employer values your talents, it is likely that they will be happy to discuss openly why they feel the clause is included, and a compromise can be reached.

If you do find yourself in any doubt over a legal topic or with anything concerning your contract with an employer, consult a legal expert who has experience working with creative professionals. These topics also prompt endless discussion on the web, if you wish to listen in.

bmitted for
ng leading to
Web Hosting

ind uses
nography,
racy,
y illegal
n illegal
rivacy..

indemnify,
mless from
osses, costs

e Design
web site. This
ist
s, its clients,

2//

15. Ownership to Web Pages and Graphics.
Copyright to the finished assembled work of web pages and graphics produced by shall be vested with the Client upon final payment for the project. This ownership is to include, design, photos, graphics, source code, work-up files, text, and any program(s) specifically designed or purchased on behalf of the Client for completion of this project.

Rights to photos, graphics, computer programs are specifically not transferred to the Client, and remain the property of their respective owners. and its subcontractors retain the right to display all designs as examples of their work in their respective portfolios.

16. Payment of Fees.
A minimum deposit of twenty five percent (25%) is required to commence work.

payment of $

The undersig
agreement o
or business.

On behalf of
(authorized s

_____

_____ Dat

On behalf of
(authorized s

_____

1// *Your portfolio is a record of your past employment. Just like a resumé, you rely on it to get new work.*

2// *Example of a design studio's contract with a client that specifically provides for future display of the project in their portfolio.*

Copyright law: protecting your work

1//

Copyright ©2009 The Norik.
All rights reserved.

JOHNNY DOES - ALL RIGHTS RESERVED © 2009

2//

International copyright law is a broad topic that relates not only to visual creativity, but also to writing, music, and more. The law is there to govern what other people can and cannot do with your work and to protect your right of ownership of your work as a creative professional.

Unfortunately, putting your portfolio on the web introduces certain risks, namely more exposure to those willing to violate your copyright. It is therefore a good idea to spend a little time finding out exactly what your rights are as the original creator of the work so that you can act immediately if you suspect someone has attempted to reproduce your personal work in any way.

What follows is some general information about your rights. It is important to note that this book is not intended as a comprehensive guide to copyright law nor as a substitute for professional legal advice. If you have serious questions about the legalities surrounding creative ownership, seek the advice of a legal expert.

You may wish to supplement the information in this book with your own research. There are many helpful sources of copyright law information on the web. Five good starting points are:

- United States Copyright Office: copyright.gov
- European Copyright Office: eucopyright.com
- Intellectual Property Office of New Zealand:
  www.iponz.govt.nz/cms/copyright
- Australian Copyright Council: www.copyright.org.au
- Creative Commons: creativecommons.org

Your rights in summary:

If you create a unique piece of work and you did not create it for an employer or client under a contract that states that they own the copyright for that work, you automatically have copyright protection for it. Note that the work is copyright-protected by standardized international law regardless of whether or not you place the copyright symbol and your name on or near the work.

Copyright as a form of intellectual property ownership means you have the right to publish and distribute the creative work as you see fit. It also means you have the right to create derivative works and adaptations of the original without restriction. You may also assign the copyright to others.

If you have done work for an employer or client under a contract that states that they have the copyright to that work, refer to pages 128–129, where you will find recommendations regarding showing work done for a previous employer.

To find out if your images are being reproduced anywhere on the web, there are services offering subscription-fee accounts at a range of price points to which you can upload your images so that its software can scan the web for reproductions and report back to you.

Your hosting provider's usage statistics can also help you see if anyone is including references to your image files on their pages. View the stats to see if any individual image files have been requested a disproportionate number of times. A search on that file name may lead you to discover an illegal placement of that image in someone else's site.

1// *The copyright symbol.*

2// *Notice of copyright is not required for copyright ownership to exist. It is, however, an opportunity to state the name of the copyright owner.*

1//

The copyright realm of the overall intellectual property landscape is a constantly shifting one filled with endless litigious debate over various areas open to interpretation. However, the fundamental rules of copyright law are clear and can be enforced. Here are answers to some common questions:

Q: Do I need to have a copyright notice on or near my work for my copyright to be valid?

A: No, you do not need to display a copyright notice on or near your work for your copyright to be valid. The Berne Convention, agreed to by a majority of countries, gives automatic copyright on creations whether that copyright is registered or not, and notice of copyright is not required. It is not a bad idea to display your copyright information, however, as it helps remove any potential ambiguity over copyright ownership.

Q: Do I need to register my copyright?

A: You do not need to register your copyright for it to be valid. Registration is a good idea if you have a piece that you think is at particular risk, as it allows for certain benefits such as the ability to recoup more costs in the case of legal action.

Q: How do I register my copyright?

A: Copyright registration in the United States can be performed online via the US Copyright Office website at copyright.gov. In Europe and elsewhere there are various services that provide copyright registration. Learn more about registration at eucopyright.com (Europe), www.iponz.govt.nz/cms/copyright (New Zealand), and www.copyright.org.au (Australia).

Q: Someone is violating my copyright. What can I do?

A: Make sure they definitely know that they have violated your copyright. Contact them to tell them to stop using your material. If they clearly know that they are violating your copyright and continue doing so, you should obtain some legal advice. There are a number of tactics that can be employed from this point, such as contacting the violator's internet service provider, but if you are wary of getting in over your head it might be best to get professional advice before taking action.

2//

Q: Someone has created something that is a parody of a creation of mine. Have they violated my copyright?

A: Possibly not. If their use of your work can be defined as a transformative parody, it may be defendable under fair use or fair dealing legislation. To learn more about fair use, refer to the information on pages 134–135.

Q: What is a Creative Commons license?

A: It is a form of copyright protection provided by the non-profit organization Creative Commons. In their own words, "The Creative Commons licenses enable people to easily change their copyright terms from the default of 'all rights reserved' to 'some rights reserved'." You may choose to allow others to use a piece from your portfolio with attribution by attaching a Creative Commons license to it. Examples of many Creative Commons assets can be found on sites such as Flickr. Learn more at creativecommons.org.

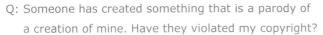

1// *Creative Commons images on Flickr.*

2// *creativecommons.org, the home of the non-profit corporation, Creative Commons.*

Derivative work and fair use

1//2//

Derivative work is created by taking an existing piece and adapting it to create something new, but with identifiable elements of the original. Examples are as far-ranging as movie adaptations of books, Marcel Duchamp's *L.H.O.O.Q.* (an image of Leonardo's Mona Lisa with a scrawled-on mustache and beard), and the musical *West Side Story* (derivative of Shakespeare's play *Romeo and Juliet*).

If someone creates a piece of work that appears to be derivative of a creation of yours, have they violated your copyright? To answer this for any particular case, the concept of "transformativeness" becomes very important. If someone has created a derivative work based on your original, is there something transformative about the end result? Is there some insight that viewers of the new work will gain about your original? If yes, they may have a defendable case for creating something that is derivative of your work without express permission from you.

Moral rights as provided for in most countries require that, as the original creator, you be given clear attribution for your work and that you have the right to remove your name from a derivative piece if you don't like it. For example, if you transfer copyright to another person with the caveat that the work cannot be used for certain purposes (for example, advertising a product you do not wish to be associated with) and that caveat is not adhered to, you may have legal grounds to do something about it.

Fair use (in the US) and fair dealing (in several Commonwealth countries) are terms used to describe a doctrine of copyright exceptions under which one can take certain liberties with copyright restrictions and hold a defendable position.

Fair use is based on a four-factor assessment system.
If a copyright is believed to be infringed and fair use is used
as a defense, the court will have to assess on the basis of:

1. the purpose and character of the use;
2. the nature of the copyrighted work;
3. the amount and substantiality of the portion used
   in relation to the copyrighted work as a whole; and
4. the effect of the use upon the potential market
   for or value of the copyrighted work.[1]

Fair dealing, based on similar concepts, varies from country
to country. There are allowances for use of copyrighted material
without permission for some or all of the following uses, with
some exceptions:

- research and study;
- review and critique;
- parody and satire;
- news reportage; and
- giving of professional advice.

In one of the more famous fair use cases, the publisher of
Roy Orbison's "Pretty Woman" sued 2 Live Crew for copyright
infringement for their song "Oh, Pretty Woman." The song was
deemed to be a parody of the original by the Supreme Court
and therefore allowable under fair use law, the point being that
the song formed a ridiculing commentary that itself became
an original product.

L.H.O.O.Q.

3//

1//2// *The musical* West Side Story
(top image) is a derivative work of
Shakespeare's Romeo and Juliet
(lower image).
*(*West Side Story*) © Tessa Watson*
flickr.com/photos/tessawatson
creativecommons.org/licenses/by/2.0
*(*Romeo and Juliet*) © Ygor Oliveira*
flickr.com/photos/-ygor
creativecommons.org/licenses/by/2.0

3// *Marcel Duchamp's* L.H.O.O.Q.
is a derivative work of Leonardo
da Vinci's Mona Lisa.

1. US CODE: Title 17,107. Limitations on exclusive rights: Fair use
   http://www4.law.cornell.edu/uscode/17/107.html

Crediting collaborators

When your portfolio contains elements that other people created, whether as content that is contained within your work or as part of a collaboration, it is ethically responsible to credit those contributors. In addition to showing respect, it has the added benefit of helping clarify what you did and didn't contribute to the project.

In the case of a collaborative project, consider listing the entire team that worked on the project along with their roles, and highlight yourself in the list. This approach is particularly useful for reviewers who are interested in getting a sense of the size of the teams you have worked with and how many hats you have worn.

A clean and simple place to locate credits is embedded in the project description area associated with each piece of work you display. In this way the list of names and roles will augment your own role description. Remember to provide credit to a collaborator in the footer of your entire site if you have had someone's significant help in building it.

1//

2//

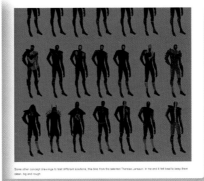

The days where very intense. Over 130 people where on the call-sheet. Cameraman David Grehn, Skellefteå, is focused.

Some other concept drawings to test different solutions, this time from the talented Therese Larsson. In the end it felt best to keep them clean, big and rough.

3//

If the individuals you are crediting have portfolio sites as well, the logical step is to provide links to their sites where you give them credit. Ideally, they will reciprocate, and overall business by referral should increase.

Note that most copyright law provides for some moral rights provisions that may require clear attribution of creative authorship regardless of economic ownership, so in many cases you not only have a moral obligation to provide a credit, it may be technically illegal not to. Put in simpler terms: a creator may have the right to be credited whether they are the copyright owner of that piece or not.

If a designer does the unthinkable and tries to take credit for someone else's work, the design community will likely prove itself quite small and well networked. Making false claims and doing wrong by others is very likely to come back in a reputation-damaging way.

1// *Nelson Balaban,*
xtrabold.net
Example of crediting in the
case of a collaboration.

2// *25ah, 25ah.se*
In this example, the agency,
photographer, and stylist
are credited.

3// *Robert Lindström, Designchapel,*
designchapel.com
In a blog post about the making of
Teamgeist, North Kingdom art director
and co-founder Robert Lindström
gives detailed crediting information
regarding individual contributors.

Gallery

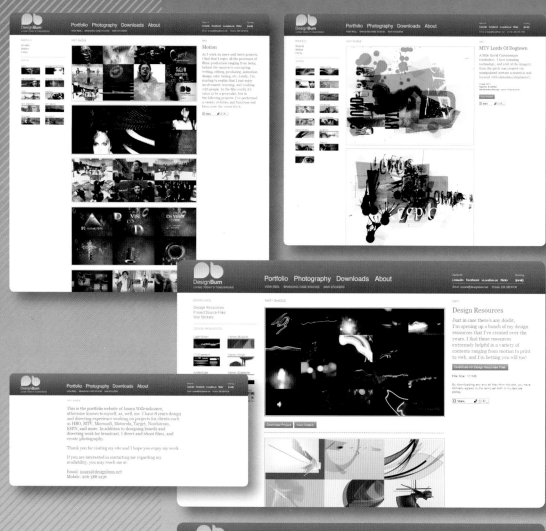

Designbum, Issara Willenskomer,

designbum.net

Direction, motion design,

and photography

Seattle, US

Combination of list and gallery format.

This is a website.

A seventh iteration of iamalwayshungry representing a bulk of work from 2008 and some of 2009 in a temporary and experimental shell.

Click and drag to navigate.
Use tabs to the left and right or arrow keys to navigate quickly.

The previous site lives here

Nessim Higson,
iamalwayshungry.com
Design and art direction
Alabama, US
Conceptual format
(multidirectional scrolling).

Gallery

Nick Jones, narrowdesign.com
Flash design and development, art
direction, and web design
Minneapolis, US
List navigation format.

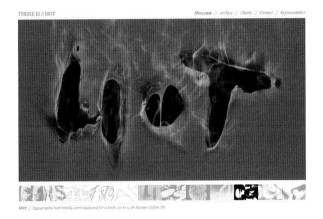

THERE IS // HOT

HOT // Typographic test initially commissioned for a book cover with Harper Collins NY.

Sean Freeman, thereis.co.uk

Typographic illustration

UK

Gallery format.

THERE IS // CREAM 09

CREAM 09 // Artwork for an invitation to Cream; an event showcasing the top 20 graduate creative teams from around the world all under one roof.

Gallery

Serial Cut, serialcut.com

Art direction

Madrid, Spain

List navigation format.

Qube Konstrukt, qubekonstrukt.com

Design studio

Melbourne, Australia

List navigation format.

Chapter Five:
Launching your portfolio

Chapter Six:
Getting the most from your portfolio

GOING LIVE

Getting ready to launch is an exciting time. Make sure you get the most from your portfolio by testing it thoroughly, being open to feedback, and trying to connect with potential clients and employers in the most effective ways.

When it comes to presenting your new digital portfolio, there are several techniques and guidelines that can be helpful in putting your best foot forward. Self-promotional tactics and how to handle following up are critical areas for generating real and sustained interest in your creative work.

CHAPTER FIVE: Launching your portfolio
The soft launch

1//

Going live with your new portfolio site is an exciting time. All of that hard effort is about to pay off. Quite often people find themselves needing to get a site live in a hurry. Maybe you have an important interview lined up, or an award submission deadline. Whatever your reason, hopefully you can find a little extra time for refinement by considering a soft launch.

Soft launching a site means making it live without promoting it in any way. One practical way to pull this off is to have a usable version of your portfolio available already, perhaps using one of the free services reviewed in Chapter Two, and keep using that as your primary portfolio as you quietly launch your new one in order to get feedback from select colleagues and friends. This approach allows you to test your site thoroughly for issues such as usability bugs and technical glitches, as well as collecting useful feedback.

The soft launch is a common approach in website development. Often referred to in two stages as a site's "alpha" and "beta" phases, the technique is testament to the fact that websites are complicated and you need help identifying potential issues and room for improvement.

Follow the advice on the next few pages for testing and collecting feedback to make sure that when you put the full force of promotion behind your site you'll really be putting your best foot forward.

Tech tip

When your new site is a redesign of an existing portfolio, a common practice is to soft launch your site in a folder off your root folder, such that your new site is hidden from view but available to those you direct to it. For example, put your entire new site in a folder called "new" and it will be available to a select few of your choosing at "[yourwebaddress]/new."

2//

1// Fudge, madebyfudge.com
An example of clever conceptual
messaging indicating a work
in progress.

2// Billy Tamplin, billytamplin.com
A blog post announcing the launch
of a new site.

Test the site thoroughly

1//

It is surprising how easy it is to view a website many times over and still miss the most basic mistakes. It is important to realize that as a visual designer or artist and not a trained interaction designer with quality assurance experience, you are biased toward focusing on the appearance of your site and not necessarily all of its inner workings.

Thorough testing is about predicting the common tasks your target audience will want to perform and then faithfully recreating them to assess the experience. A basic example of a suitable test plan might be for the tester to perform the following steps and make notes along the way:

1. Visit homepage
2. Find examples of illustration work
3. Browse at least five pieces
4. Read bio
5. Read resumé
6. Make contact

A simple test plan such as this will help highlight answers to questions such as:

1. Do the pages load quickly and easily?
2. Is the primary navigation clear and easy to use?
3. Is the secondary navigation clear and is it easy to move through the work?
4. Is information about you easy to find and read?
5. Is your work experience easy to find and read?
6. Is contact information or a contact form easy to find and use? Does the contact form work and is its functionality intuitive?

Some common pitfalls visual designers fall victim to when taking on interaction design include:

- The text is too small to read in body content and navigation.
- The contact form looks great but is difficult to use due to overcustomization; it does not allow for a long enough message.
- The site takes too long to load because the overall file sizes are too large.
- There are issues with too much complex Flash animation and it makes one's computer chug, resulting in poor motion frame rate.

Asking an objective person to perform testing is a good idea for unearthing problems you might not find yourself because you know the site so well. Grab a friend or colleague, set them down in front of the site with no prior knowledge, and give them a set of tasks to perform. Ask them to think out loud to gain extra information about what is going through their head as they perform tasks.

Remember to test your site on all the popular web browsers (Internet Explorer, Firefox, Safari, and Chrome) and on different platforms (Mac and PC). Some custom-built sites can look very different depending on the viewing software specification.

Tech tip

Fivesecondtest at fivesecondtest.com is a helpful free service for crowdsourcing basic usability tests. Upload design mockups and set up click tests and memory tests. Invite friends or colleagues to participate or simply get test data from passersby.

For a more comprehensive web-based user testing service, check out Loop11 at loop11.com. You must pay for this service after the free trial runs out.

1// *Fivesecondtest,*
fivesecondtest.com
Example of a simple click test.

Get feedback

Experienced designers and artists know that the ability to take feedback well and use it constructively is a valuable skill. Don't be afraid to put the right audience in front of your site and ask them to be honest about what they think. Give them every indication that you want their real opinion and can handle it. Explain that you are in a position to pause and reflect on your work now and can do something to integrate helpful feedback, so it's the perfect time for them to be forthcoming.

Don't always expect the best feedback to come immediately while you're reviewing the site with someone. Consider giving them the opportunity to review it on their own and reflect on their thoughts before getting back to you. Giving them an opportunity to find the words for their constructive feedback without being rushed should result in better-quality feedback.

1//

2//

Tech tip

Like usability testing, feedback gathering can be crowdsourced using services such as Concept Feedback at conceptfeedback.com. Sign up for a free account and upload imagery or mockups of your site. Members of the Concept Feedback community will provide detailed feedback. Reviewers have reputation ratings that help you prioritize their feedback.

When interviewing with prospective employers, if you feel it is appropriate and you have a good rapport, consider inviting the reviewer to check out your new site and give you some honest feedback. This invitation, if delivered in the right way, will not only bring you valuable feedback from your target audience, it may also impress your potential employers with the depth of your ambition and confidence.

If you are a student, be sure to seek the opinions of faculty and peers whose perspective you value. Learn to spot good and bad feedback. Bad feedback-givers tell you what they think you want to hear. Good feedback-givers are straightforward, honest, but also constructive. They will give you their genuine impression without focusing too much on solutions and back-seat art directing.

Keep an eye out for professional portfolio review opportunities such as open studios and other industry events.

1// *Concept Feedback,*
conceptfeedback.com

2// *Get Satisfaction,*
getsatisfaction.com
Placing a feedback tab on your site
via services such as Get Satisfaction
at getsatisfaction.com can be another
good way to collect helpful ideas for
improving your site.

Connecting with potential employers

To get meetings with your target employers and clients, be proactive, confident, and persistent. Being proactive and organized may mean making a list of all the places at which you are interested in working or all the potential clients you would like to have. Start doing your homework from one end of the list to the other. A spreadsheet can be a good tool to help manage this process.

Visit each company's website to collect important information such as email addresses and the names of any key people you believe you may need to reach. Does their website advertise any positions you would be a match for? If so, seize the opportunity straight away.

If there aren't any job ads on the site, consider calling the main number to ask if the company is hiring. If they put you through directly to a manager, that is rare but a good thing, so be prepared to give a brief elevator pitch. Chances are they will just give you an email address to send your details to, but if they are urgently trying to fill a position that matches your pitch they may make special considerations.

Check jobs database websites and apply for as many relevant positions as you care to. Consider taking on as many interviews as you can during your search, both for practice and information gathering. You can always back out later on if you decide the role is not for you.

1//

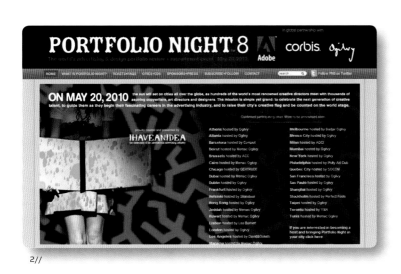

2//

Q: What works when it comes to getting through to you for an interview?

"What gets my attention is an individual with passion—not just for their own work but for the company they want to work at and their industry overall."
—Iain McDonald, Founder, Amnesia Razorfish, Australia

There is nothing wrong with contacting as many businesses as you're attracted to and expressing interest in working for them. Do your homework by learning as much as you can about each company from their websites and the press. Use this insight to your advantage by asking informed questions that get you closer to your target audience.

Cast a wide net and you will get better results overall than if you choose your one favorite employer, aim for your dream job, and get turned down.

Attend industry conferences and seminars and make a point of asking relevant questions of the speakers and moderators. These are quite often the same individuals you will be trying to get work from.

1// Design conference
Semi-Permanent, semipermanent.com
Industry conferences and seminars can be good opportunities to network and find employment opportunities.

2// Portfolio Night,
portfolionight.com
Portfolio Night is an international event for aspiring advertising creatives—an opportunity to meet creative directors and receive valuable advice and feedback.

Presenting your portfolio in person

1//

Presenting in person is always preferable to presenting over the phone or by other means. There are some subtleties of communication that cannot be conveyed without eye contact and the ability to read body language.

In person you have the ability to change the pace of your presentation if necessary, and you can choose what to show based on reviewer feedback or the cues you pick up about their work environment and mood.

Just as you value a portfolio that is visually impressive, consider your appearance before visiting a potential client or employer. Overdressing can be just as bad as a sloppy appearance. Imagine what the employer's environment is like from a work dress standpoint and choose from your wardrobe what best matches or complements it.

Other fundamental presentation tips to keep in mind are:

Be prepared. If you have questions about the employer or client, jot them down beforehand and be ready for the discussion. Do your homework about their business and have some thoughts and comments in mind. For more on questions to ask, refer to that topic later in this chapter.

Be on time. Turning up late for a meeting says two things: that you're disorganized, and that you don't have as much respect for your reviewer's time as you should if you're hoping to get their work.

Be friendly and positive. If you are normally a gloomy person, do what you can, but know that it's a big ask for an employer to hire someone who appears to have a negative attitude. Smile, make eye contact, and be warm.

2//

Tech tip

If you are unsure whether you will have an internet connection at your interview, keep a local copy of your portfolio site on your laptop so you are ready regardless.

How does an online portfolio play into an in-person review? One way is to take a laptop to the interview and demonstrate your work via a walkthrough of your website. It gives the reviewer a chance to see how your site works so when they take a closer look later they will already be familiar with it.

If your creative output has a tangible element to it, such as printed materials, you could show the digital portfolio first and then the printed pieces in a physical portfolio. This approach shows your skills in working across a range of output types.

Ask for feedback in your review and use the reviewer's perspective to help you improve your portfolio. Their experience reviewing portfolios means they know what works.

1// Sean Ball,
behance.net/seanballdesign
Sean Ball's self-promotional CD
package contains his portfolio,
resumé, and business card, while
each metal case is wrapped in
an eye-catching sleeve.

2// Deronzier Quentin,
behance.net/neels
Having a laptop that is also a creative
conversation piece can be an asset in
a portfolio presentation.

Presenting over the phone

If you are looking for work remotely and need to walk someone through your portfolio over the phone, some of the same guidelines already covered still apply.

It's good to be prepared. Make sure you're available for the call on time and that the reviewer has the web address of your portfolio in their email inbox already. This is one instance where it's helpful to have a short, clean, web address in case they don't receive your email or if for any other reason you need to tell someone verbally how to get to your site. Keep a notepad and pen at hand for taking notes on topics such as additional work they might like to see that you'll need to send to them later.

Whether presenting over the phone or in person, it is a good idea to give relatively succinct answers. A reviewer may be put off if you talk too much. Among other problems, it will make them not want to ask you many questions. A better approach is to keep the door open for them to dive deep only on the topics they choose to ask you more about.

As you can't see what they're looking at, you may need to ask them from time to time whether they're seeing what you think they're seeing. You could arrange it so you both arrive at the main view of a project at the same time and then allow them to click through the detail views while you briefly describe your role on that project and anything particularly interesting about it.

1//

2//

Tech tip

Skype provides free video calls if you and the reviewer both have webcams and Skype accounts. It is worth considering if you think your reviewer may already be oriented toward that type of communication. It allows for a remote interview with some benefits of meeting in person. Google's competition to Skype, Google Talk, can be downloaded from google.com/talk.

Don't be afraid to slow down and pause to form your thoughts as needed. The reviewer has something to look at so a moment of silence shouldn't be a problem. Staying relaxed will help you avoid the tendency to get overexcited and talk too fast.

Similar to meeting in person, a positive attitude is important when trying to make a good impression. One trick is to remember to smile when you're talking on the phone. It can help put you in a relaxed, positive, state of mind and your voice will actually sound more upbeat.

1// *Skype, skype.com*

2// *Google Talk, google.com/talk*

Discussing your work

1//

2//

The beauty of a portfolio is that you can choose only the projects you think are relevant to the discussion you're having. Be prepared to talk about your role in each project and other important information. There are a few things that anyone will want to know when looking at your work. This list is nearly identical to the structure of the descriptions we designed into our portfolio project displays in Chapters One and Two. Use it as a guide of good points to touch on:

1. Project title and client name
2. Your role
3. The brief
4. Key insight and the basis for your solution
5. The end result

Try to avoid slipping into a monotonous voice, and aim to weave your projects together as if you are telling a story. A seamless tale from one piece to the next helps avoid dead ends and silences.

A good story can be interrupted and resumed without any trouble, so remember to invite sidetracks if the reviewer has a question that takes both of you down a different path. It is far more important to have a discussion that is relevant to both of you than for you to be unhindered while delivering your monologue.

If it's all feeling too much like a train moving from station A to station B, drop in a few funny or interesting stories related to your experience.

If you are speaking with a prospective employer, be prepared to discuss your long-term ambitions. For a business to decide to invest time in making you part of the team, they will want to know that you are intent on self-improvement and are doing the best work you can to achieve your goals. Here are some questions you may be asked when interviewing for a permanent position:

"What is your greatest strength? Your greatest weakness?"

Be prepared for this and think of a strength that might relate to the job you are there to discuss. Choose a weakness that you have a handle on and for which you are working on solutions. This will demonstrate your self-awareness and ambitions toward improvement.

"Where do you see yourself in a year's time? Five years?"

Prepare for this by finding out what inspires you and projecting forward in time. If you are stuck, find portfolios of creative people you admire, analyze their work and information, and reverse-engineer that into a story about where you want to be in the future. Be specific, but make it achievable.

"Why do you want to work here?"

Try answering this question by demonstrating some unique information about the business that attracts you. This also gives you a chance to pay the company a compliment.

3//

1// *Corking Design, Daniel Cork, corkingdesign.co.uk*

Daniel's description of this personal project is very conversational; it is appropriately descriptive but concise, positive, and relaxed.

2// *Sreski, Mark Dormand, sreski.com*

Constructing an "about" page such as this can be excellent preparation for interviews. It can serve as the rough script of your presentation, from which you can divert and return to.

3// *Orman Clark, ormanclark.com*

Remember to be direct when describing what you do—a list of the services you provide, as in this example, can be good to state if it's not already obvious.

Questions to ask in interviews

Asking good questions in an interview or business meeting achieves three key things:

1. Good questions create good answers. The knowledge you gain will benefit you later.
2. You can demonstrate that you have done your homework and are interested in the business and the individual.
3. You can communicate that you are evaluating your interviewers just as they are evaluating you. This is a two-way dialog, so asking the right questions can help level up the perceived power balance to some degree.

The exact questions you ask will depend on your situation and the homework you do, but here are some common questions that can lead to interesting information and discussion. General questions to ask employers of creative professionals when seeking contract work or permanent employment:

"What's a day in the life like for the role you're trying to fill?"

"What's your favorite project the company has worked on/ delivered in recent memory and why?"

"What, in your opinion, is the company's crowning achievement?"

"How do you describe what the company does when pressed to do so in as few words as possible?"

"What is the single most exciting creative trend or innovation that the company has its eye on at the moment?"

"Who do you consider to be your competition and what companies do you admire?"

1//

These questions are all conversation starters and typically can't be answered with one or two words. Getting them talking is a good thing. Practice being a good listener and take it all in.

The following questions are not great to ask unless you can't get the information any other way; they are not open-ended and may make it seem that you haven't done your homework:

"Who are your clients?"

"What services do you provide?"

"How many employees do you have?"

"Is this your only office location?"

"What is the job description?"

General questions to ask prospective direct clients if you are a freelance creative professional:

"What's the problem we're trying to solve?"

"When you think of this brief, what are some brands and products that you think are good reference points?"

"What's the single most important thing we need to accomplish/communicate?"

"Who will be my main point of contact and how will the project be managed?"

"What existing brand elements, guidelines, and considerations do I need to become familiar with?"

2//

1// behance.net/gallery/
status-calendar/203964
Burak Kaynak and cemhas.com
ask the question, "What are you
doing today?"

2// vimeo.com/jrcanest
Jr. Canest asks one of the most
important questions, "What
matters to you?"

Self-promotional leave-behinds

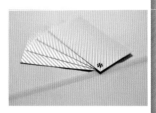

1//

Knowledge of your target audience should give you an idea of how much they might value the creativity apparent in any self-promotional elements that you leave behind after a presentation.

A well-designed business card is a good asset for any professional. For illustrators, photographers, and other creatives, a printed card with a collage of work is a standard technique for leaving reviewers with a visual reference they can add to their files. This piece is often referred to as the "leave-behind."

There are many excellent examples of creative approaches to leave-behinds. If you want to stand out from the crowd, consider your development of self-promotional pieces like any creative challenge; begin by identifying the problem to be solved and brainstorm on solutions. Be sure to source plenty of inspiration by searching on keywords like "self-promotion" on design networks such as Behance.

Of course, leave-behinds can come in digital form as well. A CD or DVD containing digital files and decorated with a printed label reflecting your identity is one option. The contents of the disk would most likely be a showcase of your work in some form—either a navigable multimedia experience, a PDF document, a motion reel, or all of the above. If the contents are simply a reproduction of your website without any additional value, there is probably not much reason to go down this route.

Small, removable, storage devices can be branded on the outside with your identity and house the same types of files you might burn onto a CD.

We wanted to get our clients moving behind their desk, so we've made up this notebook with on one side space to write and on the other side ball patterns. Just crumble up a piece of paper an you can play soccer, or rugby, or throw a tennis ball in your waste basket.
We've won a bronze medal for 'printed self promotion' in 2007 European Design Awards for this design
You can purchase the notebook via our little web-shop on www.trappedinsuburbia.com

3//

2//

1// *Hayden Miller, hmillerdesign.com*
A well-designed business card and
resumé are essential for a print-
oriented graphic designer.

2// *Trapped in Suburbia,*
trappedinsuburbia.com
Clients are invited to "play more"
with this cleverly designed notepad.

3// *Alexandra Dobra,*
behance.net/alexandradobra
CD leave-behinds look most
professional when both the insert and
the label are purposefully designed.

Following up after interviews

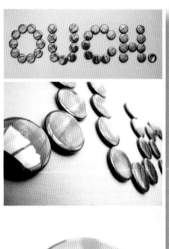
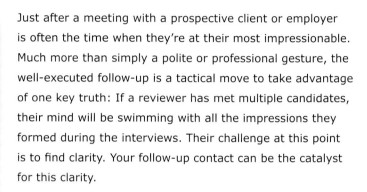

Just after a meeting with a prospective client or employer is often the time when they're at their most impressionable. Much more than simply a polite or professional gesture, the well-executed follow-up is a tactical move to take advantage of one key truth: If a reviewer has met multiple candidates, their mind will be swimming with all the impressions they formed during the interviews. Their challenge at this point is to find clarity. Your follow-up contact can be the catalyst for this clarity.

The bare minimum should be a thank-you email, ideally delivered later that day or at worst within 24 hours. Be sure to thank the reviewer for their time and provide any additional information or work samples they may have requested. This is also a good opportunity to reassert your contact details, including the address of your online portfolio.

After that, it's a good idea to follow up again about a week after the point at which they said they'd be getting back to you with a decision. This gives them time to run a bit late with the decision if they need to without feeling pestered. Checking back at this time will help reestablish your interest and keep you on their radar.

Keeping in touch by sending them links and information you think they might find interesting based on conversations you may have had can be effective for keeping contact as well. However, be wary of overdoing this, as clogged inboxes are a key irritation in today's hectic workplace.

1//

If you do freelance work and you are looking to follow up after a potential new business meeting, consider going a step further than the email thank-you alone. A custom-made or templated landing page for your portfolio can be an effective way to show your potential new client that you value their time and want to put all of the relevant information for them in one easy-to-access location. It will also demonstrate your ability to present ideas and information clearly and practically—an attractive quality for businesses looking to hire creative professionals.

To achieve this, design and build a standalone page off your main web address and consider filling it with the following elements:

- Your thank-you letter.
- Specific links to work within your portfolio relevant to the meeting you had.
- Any additional information or work links as discussed in the meeting.
- Your contact information.

Turn the page into a template you can use on other potential clients and you can streamline the entire process.

There are many ways to get creative with this approach. The more you impress with a follow-up technique, the more you can increase your chances of getting hired.

2//

1// Sarah France, sarahfrance.com
Sarah France leaves behind a button that states the obvious but true "Sarah France gave me this."

2// Scott Buschkuhl, hinterlandstudio.com
Scott's mini-portfolio pamphlets make an excellent leave-behind.

CHAPTER SIX: Getting the most from your portfolio
Stand out from the crowd

1//

The best, most reliable, most foolproof way to stand out from the crowd is to do very good work and make sure it shows in your portfolio. This is where developing new work for your portfolio may become important. If you feel your body of work is lacking somehow, do something about it. Invent fake briefs and self-promotional challenges for yourself. For more ideas on this, refer back to Chapter Three.

We talked about creating your portfolio in a flexible way so you can optimize the mix of content for each meeting. Do this effectively and you may stand out by sheer relevance. Shuffle more relevant pieces to the front and place the rest in the equivalent of an appendix. If doing this leaves your best work out, reevaluate the mix and adjust until the balance feels right.

Another way to impress and be noticed is to be active in the design community; join organizations, blog frequently, enter competitions, and collaborate with colleagues on projects for fun. Finding the right voice for talking about these qualities in a meeting can do a lot for fleshing out your complete story.

Highly conceptual online portfolios are one way to differentiate yourself. Certainly when compared to very straightforward scrolling page, gallery view, and list navigation content frameworks as discussed in Chapter Two, portfolio sites designed around an original concept—a visual metaphor, a unique navigation device, or something altogether abstract but magical—can be more likely to make people take notice. Concepting and building sites such as these requires more effort and can be challenging. Fall short and you risk looking as if you have overengineered the solution. Evaluate your own risk/reward pros and cons and find the balance that suits you.

How you conduct yourself in the interview or business meeting itself is also a good opportunity to leave a lasting impression. Calmness, confidence, good eye contact, preparation, interest, and engagement... all of these qualities combined will do wonders for your image.

If you are relaxed and love what you do, you will probably be able to inject some fun and humor into the presentation of your work. If you can make someone laugh, that's a very good start.

Finally, to recap: The most important ways to leave the right impression are to have a plan, be prepared, know what you're doing so you're not in over your head, then take a deep breath and feel confident about who you are and what you do.

Q: What can people do to really get your attention?

"Someone who can design a good resumé gets my attention. It's a good indication if a designer knows typography."
—Annie Huang, Creative Director, Bocu & Bocu, Los Angeles

"Just show me strong, original work presented clearly and passionately."
—Andy Pearce, Creative Director, Amnesia Razorfish, Australia

2//

1// Reclarkgable,
reclarkgable.com
Great ideas well executed
always stand out.

2// Iain Crawford,
behance.net/iaincrawford and
iaincrawford.com
Exposure on creative social networks
such as Behance can help your
portfolio stand out.

Avoid common presentation mistakes

Here are some common mistakes when presenting a portfolio and some suggestions on how to avoid them:

- Don't be clueless about the role and the company.
  Do your homework. Review the company's website and what people are saying about them.

- Don't get lost on your way to a meeting and don't be late.
  Be prepared ahead of time with adequate directions and aim to get to the area early. Get a coffee so you only have to stroll across the road.

- Don't rely on the reviewer having a computer or an internet connection you can access.
  Have your entire portfolio site or simply your work samples available on a laptop without needing an internet connection.

- Don't talk too fast or give excessively long answers to questions.
  Relax. Breathe calmly. Give relatively short answers to questions. Allow the reviewer to talk and listen intently.

- Don't be overly negative about past employers as it may reveal that you're a magnet for controversy.
  Do discuss past situations in terms of challenges and the steps you took to put in place solutions to overcome them. Emphasize the positive.

- Don't forget that you are the one driving the presentation of your portfolio.
  Be the one to set the pace and tell your story.

Some general advice on setting appropriate expectations mentally:

It's easy to get your hopes up about the outcome of an interview or business meeting. If you don't get the job, it can be disheartening and a challenge to not take it personally. Try to avoid the rejection rollercoaster ride by setting appropriate expectations for yourself ahead of an interview.

The challenge is to feel confident enough in the meeting (an emotional high), but not to set yourself up for crashing if you don't get the job (an emotional low). The answer lies in preparation, the power of casting a wide net, and a zen-like grasp of calm confidence.

1//

Here is a demonstration of two ways to prepare for an interview:

Mental scenario A: "I really want this job. Actually, I need this job. It is the one perfect job for me. I really hope this works out and I'll be devastated if it doesn't."

Mental scenario B: "I've always been a fan of this place, and I'd really love it if I worked here one day. For now there are a lot of places I could be happy. All I'm really hoping to get out of today is to establish contact and exchange some information. I might even get some useful feedback on my portfolio."

Scenario A is a recipe for heartbreak. You're really setting yourself up for stress. Scenario B is solid because it's almost impossible to not achieve those objectives.

Nurturing an attitude that there are many places you could happily work will help greatly with your ability to be calm and confident.

Setting objectives such as establishing contact and exchanging useful information is an effective way to take small steps toward the end goal of advancing your career. The more conversations you have with senior people in your profession, the more you'll learn and the more they'll know about you.

Q: What's the most common mistake you see people make with their portfolio or in interviews?

"The most common mistake I see people make is to show too much and talk too much."
—Annie Huang, Creative Director, Bocu & Bocu, Los Angeles

"A badly ordered book is a common mistake. Start strong and finish strong and tell a story with the work."
—Andy Pearce, Creative Director, Amnesia Razorfish, Australia

1// *Don't rely on others for a computer to present your work digitally—bring your own.*
© *Travis Isaacs*
flickr.com/photos/tbisaacs
creativecommons.org/licenses/by/2.0

Self-promotion online

Raising your profile in relevant networks is a great way to increase the amount of work and creative opportunities coming through your door. Maintaining a blog, participating in a creative social network, and entering competitions are three effective ways to lift your profile online.

Enter competitions to challenge yourself and add to your portfolio. At any given time there are a massive number of competitions for all different formats across many disciplines. Have a look online by browsing the creative social networks, listening to Twitter Search, and choosing relevant tags on Delicious, the popular bookmarking service.

Join some creative social networks for exposure to feedback, collaboration, and jobs. Similar to online professional portfolio services, creative social networks allow you to create a profile for free and showcase your work. There is an emphasis on collecting friends and followers in the network and you will discover many social features in wide use, such as the ability for others to leave comments about your work.

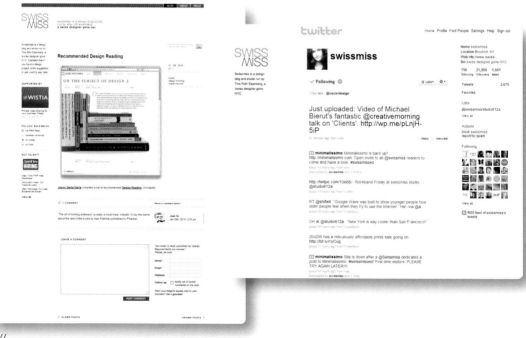

1//

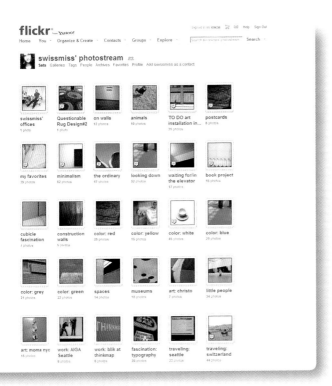

Q: How do you first hear about the portfolios that you review? How do they come to you?

"It's not just about portfolios that land on my desk—I also discover people. I like seeing great work and look for it using social channels such as Twitter, LinkedIn, blogs, etc. It's part of my job to keep my eyes open—people who make their work 'discoverable' in the social age may get an edge."
—Iain McDonald, Founder, Amnesia Razorfish, Australia

Create a profile and begin networking, sharing ideas and information, and gaining visibility with potential employers. The most popular creative social networks include Behance, Tumblr, deviantART, and Flickr.

Maintain a blog to broadcast your interests and thinking, help start conversations, and increase your site's search engine optimization. Blog platforms support images, text, and embedded video. Popular free blogging platforms include WordPress, Blogger, and Tumblr.

For more information on blogging, refer to Chapter Three.

1// *Swiss Miss, Tina Roth Eisenberg, swiss-miss.com, twitter.com/swissmiss, flickr.com/photos/swissmiss Swiss Miss is a popular design blog that began as a personal project. Tina's use of social media makes an excellent example for creative professionals to follow.*

Gallery

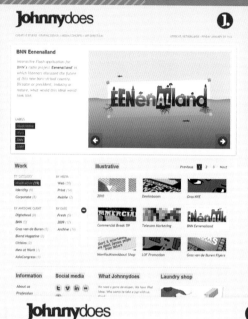

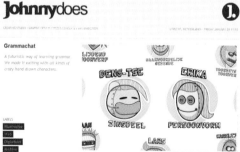

Johnnydoes, johnnydoes.nl

Graphic design, media concepts,

and art direction

Netherlands

Gallery format.

HunterGatherer

MyFace

"Stopping the Next One"

Charles & Ray Eames for Polaroid SX-70

Mollusk Old Tyme Craft Fair

00's

HunterGatherer

Video/Film   Design   Illustration   Reel   About   News

Fuel TV Signature Series
HunterGatherer

HunterGatherer

Swerve Festival

September 26-27, 2007 Los Angeles, California

HunterGatherer

Money Mark
Brand New By Tomorrow CD/LP

HunterGatherer

Video/Film   Design   Illustration   Reel   About   News

Money Mark
Brand New By Tomorrow CD/LP

HunterGatherer, huntergatherer.net

Design, illustration, animation,

and production

Brooklyn, New York City, US

Gallery format.

Gallery

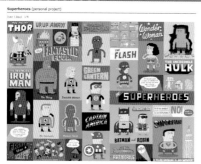

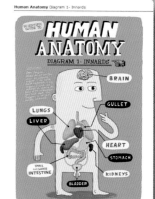

Loopland, Allan Sanders.

loopland.net

Illustration

Brighton, UK

List navigation format.

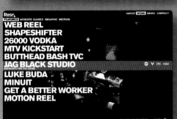

Resn, resn.co.nz

Interactive agency

New Zealand

List navigation format.

Gallery

Julia Fullerton-Batten,

juliafullerton-batten.com

Site by Bite, bitedigital.com

Photography

London, UK

List navigation format.

HENNIG OLSEN

NORWEGIAN ICECREAM BRAND
Hennig Olsen Frozen Products Catalogue.

CHECK OUT THE PROJECT IMAGES.
CLICK HERE.

NORWEGIAN WATER BA

Artwork for Local Water and Power Event

The biggest challenge I had on this image was the resolution, the size of the final print was 3 meters tall by 16 meters wide to cover a stand wall. I had worked on bigger images like the ROM project, but on this one I used many photoshop magics, and it took me 20-30 minutes each time I had to save the image. The problem was, I am addicted to save images almost every move I make, so it was a bit trick for me to complete this image and pray for any trouble happen with the machine whilst I wasn't saving the file. This project was commissioned by Siste Skrik Kommunikasjon from Oslo for the Norwegian Water BA, the local water company provider and I used many technics to create the artwork, 3D, vectorial and photoshop to mix all together and give it life.

CHECK OUT THE FULL ARTWORK. CLICK HERE.

LACAGE AUX FOLLES

Pitch artwork for the relaunch of the famous Broadway Show

Commissioned by SpotNYC an agency specialized in entertainment and responsible for the widely known visual identity for the Chicago Musical, I was invited to create 3 "sketches" of "branded ladies" for the upcoming relaunch of the LaCage Musical Show. As I work mostly digitally, the result was close to final pieces of artwork and they made part of the internal pitch among other concepts the agency presented to the client.

CHECK OUT THE PROJECT IMAGES.
CLICK HERE.

Adhemas Batista,

adhemas.com

Art direction, design, illustration,

and photography

Los Angeles, US

Single scrolling page format.

Chapter Seven:
Maintaining your portfolio

MAINTENANCE

Chapter Seven:
Maintaining your portfolio

MAINTENANCE

The launch of your site is just the beginning.
A portfolio is only as good as your last content
update, so be mindful of how often and by what
means you plan to keep your work topped up.

If your work is mainly print-based, you will
want to keep the originals well protected. We
will cover some tips on paper storage, as well
as providing information regarding the storage
and management of digital files.

CHAPTER SEVEN: Maintaining your portfolio
Uploading new work

The ease of content management of any website depends on the type of site and how it was designed and built. For portfolio services such as Krop and Behance, maintaining content is simple. Similarly, any site or blog built in WordPress is relatively easy to update.

Custom-built sites pose a different challenge. Unless a specific tool has been implemented for maintaining content, all changes will need to be made by someone knowledgeable in the fundamentals of front-end web development.

Highly conceptual sites with unique structures and navigation systems can be particularly difficult to maintain, as they generally require additional design work as well as redevelopment when content updates are made.

1//

2//

Add New Post

3//

Quick tip

To avoid spelling
mistakes, consider
writing descriptions of
your work in desktop
software that has a built-
in spellchecker such as
Microsoft Word, then
pasting from there into
your site.

It is a good idea to document your work as you complete it
in advance of your next portfolio update. Get in the habit of
setting aside mockups, photos, scans, and process documents
at the end of each project. Put these digital files in one central
location so the next time you update your site you don't need
to go hunting.

However you decide to upload new content to your site, be
sure to proof the end result carefully for spelling mistakes
and graphic glitches.

1// *Cargo Collective,*
cargocollective.com
Cargo's content-maintenance panel
is geared toward a fairly digital-savvy
audience, but allows for a high level
of customization.

2// *Carbonmade,*
carbonmade.com
Carbonmade provides a simple and
easy-to-use interface for adding new
content to your site.

3// *WordPress,*
wordpress.com
An example of an industry-standard
editor for creating a new blog post.

Protecting printed pieces

Most paper contains acid, which will cause the material to yellow and become brittle with age. To help counteract this effect, store your printed pieces horizontally separated by sheets of acid-free paper. Keep the pieces away from light and moisture.

It is very easy for printed pieces to become bent, creased, torn, or suffer dented edges if not properly protected. Protect your work from physical harm by placing it in a suitably structured container. Archival portfolio boxes and flat art storage cabinets with pullout trays are two options.

There are a number of manufacturers and sellers of paper storage receptacles and furniture, but remember to seek specifically "archival" products if you want to ensure a long life for your pieces.

Should you choose to frame any of your printed work, be mindful of how you frame it and where you hang it. Here are some tips to bear in mind when framing if you plan on doing it yourself, or if you would like some criteria to help you evaluate the quality of work from a professional framer:

- Hang the piece by attaching it to the backing board along the top only.
- Hang using hinges of Japanese rice paper attached with wheat or rice paste.
- Use 100% cotton rag matting for best assurance against the effects of acid on your printed piece.
- Use conservation-quality glass or acrylic to help filter out UV rays.
- Put in place a paper dustcover on the back to prevent dust and insects getting to the work from the back.
- Avoid hanging your work in rooms with excessive moisture or sunlight.

 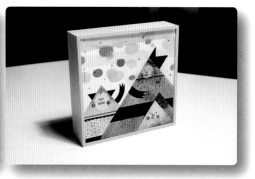

1//

2//

Digital documentation through scanning and photography are good ways to gain peace of mind. Knowing that you have an additional record of the work that you can back up in a separate location in case of fire or other damage can be comforting. Refer to Chapter Three for tips on digitizing your work.

1// Mar Hernández,

malotaprojects.com

Just one of Mar Hernández's

beautiful illustrations, thoughtfully

and simply framed.

2// 25ah,

25ah.se

An example of a complex printed

piece that could suffer damage in the

long term if not stored properly.

Storing digital files

When storing your digital files, always keep high-resolution versions of images in TIFF or very high to maximum quality JPEG format. Regardless of what resolution you output them to for various uses, you will always want to have the original, uncompressed, full-resolution source files on hand. The same principle applies with video and its various compressed file formats.

Don't apply JPEG compression to a file that has already been JPEG compressed if you can avoid it. The result will not come out as well as it would if you simply applied the same amount of compression to the original. Each time you compress an image in this way it degrades a little more.

When starting out with your first digital files, take a moment to set up a file system that will help you find particular work down the track. Consider organizing your work into folders by project placed into folders by year.

For browsing your digital files there are many software products available for download. One such product is the plugin Cool Iris, available from cooliris.com. Its 3D wall is a compellingly intuitive way to browse images and video on your local computer or the web.

1//

2//   3//

It is wise to keep your files backed up in CD or DVD format. Portable hard drives are another option. One additional benefit of having an online portfolio site is that it acts as a (low-resolution) backup of your work.

Another option is to use a web-based remote digital file storage solution such as Mozy. There are many such solutions with different features, so shop around. These services often have a small amount of storage available for free and then unlimited or a very large limit for their paid service.

1// *Cool Iris,*
cooliris.com
Image and video browsing
and search plugin.

2// *Drobo,*
drobo.com
Desktop digital file storage device.

3// *Mozy,*
mozy.com
Web-based remote digital file storage.

Resources

Design resources

24 Ways – Web design and development articles and tutorials, *24ways.org*
Abduzeedo – Graphic design inspiration and Photoshop tutorials, *abduzeedo.com*
The Artists Web – Services and information for artists online, *theartistsweb.co.uk*
Ffffound! – Image bookmarking service, *ffffound.com*
The FWA: Favorite Website Awards – Showcase of cool sites, *thefwa.com*
QBN – Design industry news and discussion, *qbn.com*
Smashing Magazine – Web design and development blog, *smashingmagazine.com*

Technical resources

Blogo – Blog publishing tool for Macs, *drinkbrainjuice.com/blogo*
Godaddy – Hosting provider, *godaddy.com*
Indexhibit – Do-it-yourself content management system, *indexhibit.org*
jQuery Plugins – Useful Javascript library, *plugins.jquery.com*
Media Temple – Hosting provider, *mediatemple.net*
Rackspace – Hosting provider, *rackspace.com and rackspace.co.uk*
TechSmith – Creators of screen capture software Snagit and Camtasia, *techsmith.com*
TopCoder – Development crowdsourcing, *topcoder.com*
Vimeo – Creative video posting community, *vimeo.com*
Webtoolkit4.me – Resources for web designers and developers, *webtoolkit4.me*
Windows Live Writer – Blog publishing tool for PCs, *download.live.com/writer*

Free services

Behance Network – Creative social network, *behance.net*
Blogger – Blogging platform, *blogger.com*
Carbonmade – Professional portfolio service, *carbonmade.com*
Cargo Collective – Professional portfolio service, *cargocollective.com*
Coroflot – Portfolio service and creative community, *coroflot.com*
deviantART Portfolio – Professional portfolio service, *portfolio.deviantart.com*
Flickr – Photography oriented social network, *flickr.com*
Krop Creative Database – Professional portfolio service, *krop.com/creativedatabase*
RedBubble – Art gallery and community, *redbubble.com*
Tumblr – Microblogging platform, *tumblr.com*
WordPress – Blogging platform, *wordpress.com*

Legalities

The Copyright Website – Copyright information and resources, *benedict.com*

Copyright – Wikipedia entry, *en.wikipedia.org/wiki/copyright*

Crash course in copyright – University of Texas website, *utsystem.edu/ogc/intellectualproperty/cprtindx.htm*

Creative Commons – Free licensing platform, *creativecommons.org*

Derivative work – Wikipedia entry, *en.wikipedia.org/wiki/derivative_work*

Digital Millennium Copyright Act – Wikipedia entry, *en.wikipedia.org/wiki/digital_millennium_copyright_act*

Fair Use of Copyrighted Materials – University of Texas website, *utsystem.edu/ogc/intellectualproperty/copypol2.htm*

Fair use – Wikipedia entry, *en.wikipedia.org/wiki/fair_use*

U.S. Copyright Office – Official government office, *copyright.gov*

Creative jobs

Behance, *behance.net/job_list*
Coroflot, *coroflot.com/public/jobs_browse.asp*
The FWA jobs, *thefwa.com/jobs*
Krop, *krop.com*
Krop jobs on Twitter, *twitter.com/krop_jobs*

People to follow on Twitter

@abduzeedo	@mlane
@behance	@qbncertified
@designerdepot	@ryancarson
@fwa	@smashingmag
@ilovetypography	@swissmiss
@ISO50	@zeldman

For further resources, see *clazie.com/digitalportfolios*

Contributors

The author and publisher would like to thank the following people for contributing images to this book:

25ah, *25ah.se*

Adam Mulyadi, *coroflot.com/public/individual_details.asp?individual_id=282174*

Adam Rix, *adamrix.com*

Adhemas Batista, *adhemas.com*

Alexandra Dobra, *behance.net/alexandradobra*

Alexey Abramov, *alexarts.ru*

Alexey Chenishov, *ftdesigner.net*

Anton Repponen, *repponen.com*

Billy Tamplin, *billytamplin.com*

Bio-bak, *bio-bak.nl*

Bonnie Jones, *bonniejonesphoto.wordpress.com*

Brianna Garcia, *briannagarcia.daportfolio.com*

Burak Kaynak and cemhas.com, *behance.net/gallery/status-calendar/203964*

Camelia Dobrin, *camellie.com*

Carsonified, *carsonified.com*

Chuck U, *chucku.com*

Corking Design, Daniel Cork, *corkingdesign.co.uk*

Danilo Rodrigues, *cargocollective.com/danilorodrigues*

Darek Nyckowiak, *thetoke.com*

Darren Whittington, *digitalvsprint.com*

Dave Werner, *okaydave.com*

David Arias, *krop.com/davidarias*

Deronzier Quentin, *behance.net/neels*

Designbum, Issara Willenskomer, *designbum.net*

Designchapel, Robert Lindström, *designchapel.com*

Kidplastik, Drew Taylor, *kidplastik.com*

Esteban Muñoz, *estebanmunoz.com*

Face, *designbyface.com*

Fat-Man Collective, *fat-man-collective.com*

Firstborn, *firstbornmultimedia.com*

Flourish Web Design, *floridaflourish.com*

Form Troopers, *formtroopers.com*

Fudge, *madebyfudge.com*

Gabrielle Rose, *drawgabbydraw.tumblr.com*

GrandArmy, *grand-army.com*

Guõmundur Bjarni Sigurõsson, *gummisig.com*

Hayden Miller, *hmillerdesign.com*

Heads of State, *theheadsofstate.com*

Hello Monday, *hellomonday.net*

HunterGatherer, Todd St. John, *huntergatherer.net*

Iain Crawford, *behance.net/iaincrawford, iaincrawford.com*

Jan Pautsch.Lilienthal, *thismortalmagic.com*

Jeff Vermeersch, *vermeersch.ca*

Jelle Gijsberts, *jellepelle.nl/archives/282*

Jessica Hische, *jessicahische.com*

Joe Bauldoff, *bauldoff.com*

Johnnydoes, *johnnydoes.nl*

JPEG Interactive, *jpeg.cn*

Jr. Canest, *vimeo.com/jrcanest*

Juan Diego Velasco, *juandiegovelasco.com*

Julia Fullerton-Batten, *juliafullerton-batten.com*

Justin Maller, *justinmaller.com*

Kareem King, *kx2web.com*

Karim Charlebois-Zariffa, *karimzariffa.com*

Kashmir Creative, Alex Antuna, *kashmircreative.com*

Kris Robinson, *oinkfu.com*

Loopland, Allan Sanders, *loopland.net*

Louise Fili, *louisefili.com*

Maciej Hajnrich, *valpnow.com, flickr.com/photos/valp00*

magneticNorth (mN), *mnatwork.com*

Marc Atlan, *krop.com/marcatlan*

Mar Hernández, *malotaprojects.com*

Marumiyan, *marumiyan.com*

Matt Titone, *matttitone.com*

Michael Kleinman, *samegoes.com*

Michele Angelo, *superexpresso.com*

Mika Mäkinen, *mcinen.net*

Mike Chan, *behance.net/mike7*

MIND Castle, *vimeo.com/8362481, mindcastleblog.com*

Monica Brand and Francisco López, *mogollon-ny.com*

Moxie Sozo, *moxiesozo.com*

Nelson Balaban, *xtrabold.net*

Nessim Higson, *iamalwayshungry.com*

New to York, Tyler Thompson, *newtoyork.com*

Nick Jones, *narrowdesign.com*

Oleg Kostuk, *theoleg.com*

Orman Clark, *ormanclark.com*

Oscar Barber, *oscarbarber.com*

Paul Lee Design, *paulleedesign.com*

Positive Hype, *positivehype.com*

Proud Creative, *proudcreative.com*

Qube Konstrukt, *qubekonstrukt.com*

Ray Sison, *skilledconcept.com*

Reclarkgable, *reclarkgable.com*

Resn, *resn.co.nz*

Ribbons of Red, *ribbonsofred.com*

Rob Palmer, *branded07.com*

Rolando Mèndez Acosta, *rolando.com.br*

Ronnie Wright, *ronniewright.co.uk*

Ryan Zunkley, *ryanzunkley.com*

Sarah France, *sarahfrance.com*

Scott Buschkuhl, *hinterlandstudio.com*

Scott Hansen, *iso50.com*

Sean Ball, *behance.net/seanballdesign*

Sean Freeman, *thereis.co.uk*

Serial Cut, *serialcut.com*

squareFACTOR, *squarefactor.com*

Sreski, Mark Dormand, *sreski.com*

Swiss Miss, Tina Roth Eisenberg, *swiss-miss.com, twitter.com/swissmiss, flickr.com/photos/swissmiss*

The Keystone Design Union, *thekdu.com*

The Norik, *thenorik.com, blog.thenorik.com*

Toby Caves, *phigerone.com*

Toothjuice, Josh Clancy, *toothjuice.net*

Toy, *toyny.com*

Trapped in Suburbia, *trappedinsuburbia.com*

Trevor Van Meter, *tvmstudio.com*

Wonderwall, *wonder-wall.com*

X Producciones Graficas, Javier Castillo, *xgraphica.com*

X3 Studios, *x3studios.com*

Zeebee Visual Communications, *zeebee.co.uk*

The author and publisher would like to thank the following people for contributing to the Employers Speak boxes:

Annie Huang, Creative Director, Bocu & Bocu, Los Angeles

Blake Kidder, Associate Creative Director, TBWA\Chiat\Day, Los Angeles

Elke Klinkhammer, Creative Director, Neue Digitale/Razorfisch, Germany

Iain McDonald, Founder, Amnesia Razorfish, Australia

Andy Pearce, Creative Director, Amnesia Razorfish, Australia

The author and publisher would like to thank the following people for contributing knowledge and insight:

Lizzie Joyce, Associate Art Director, Amnesia Razorfish

Dan Krause, Digital Designer, Amnesia Razorfish

Stephan Lange, IT Lead, Amnesia Razorfish

Sandor Moldan, Art Director, Amnesia Razorfish

Jeremy Somers, Senior Creative, Amnesia Razorfish

Index

Acknowledgments

I am grateful to the Creative Team at Amnesia Razorfish in Sydney, Australia, for their encouragement, expertise, resources, and perspective. I would also like to thank my colleagues in the UK—Isheeta Mustafi for finding me and creating the opportunity to write this book, Tony Seddon for providing his skillful art direction to bring the pages to life, and particularly my editor, Nicola Hodgson, for her guidance and insight. I'd also like to thank my wife Kirsty for all of her support and constructive feedback. This book is dedicated to my father, Ron Clazie.

About the author

Ian Clazie has worked as an interactive designer and art director in Sydney and San Francisco for fifteen years. After studying illustration and graphic design at RISD and Art Center in the early 1990s, he began his career in web design in Silicon Valley during the formative days of the worldwide web. His career has seen him work on projects as diverse as an award-winning cycling travelogue and the official website for Disney China. Most recently he managed the creative department of Razorfish Australia, where he design-directed digital projects for the likes of Pepsi, Ikea, Xbox, P&O Cruises, and Johnnie Walker. Now based in San Francisco, Ian specializes in user experience design, visual design, information architecture, design direction, and, of course, reviewing portfolios.